# THE SILVER LINK LIBRARY OF RAILWAY MODELLING

## MODELLERS' GUIDE TO THE GWR

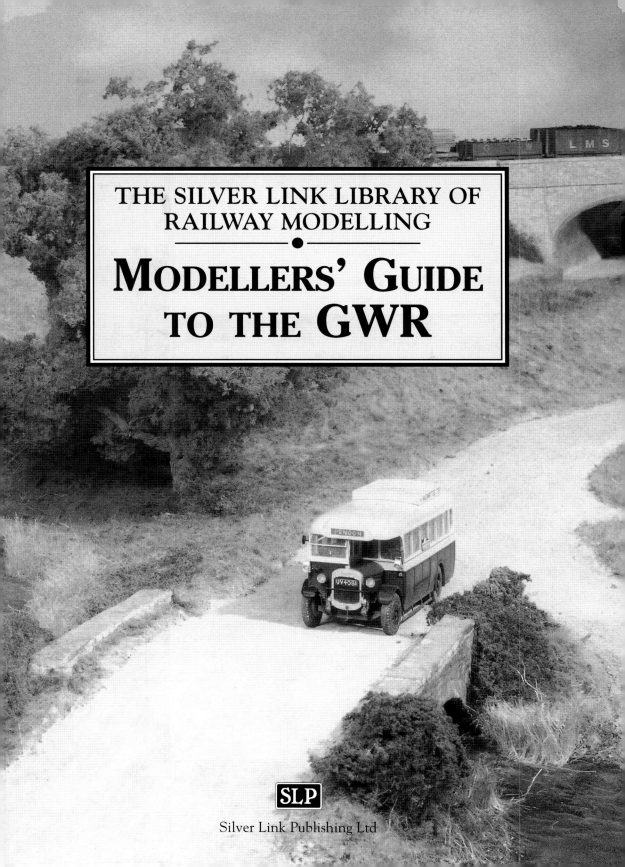

# THE SILVER LINK LIBRARY OF RAILWAY MODELLING

•

# MODELLERS' GUIDE TO THE GWR

**SLP**

Silver Link Publishing Ltd

First published by Patrick Stephens Limited in 1990
New updated and re-illustrated edition first published by Silver Link Publishing Ltd in 2002
Reprinted 2003

British Library Cataloguing in Publication Data

A catalogue record for this book is available from the British Library.

ISBN 1 85794 204 3

Silver Link Publishing Ltd
The Trundle
Ringstead Road
Great Addington
Kettering
Northants NN14 4BW

Tel/Fax: 01536 330588
email: sales@nostalgiacollection.com
Website: www.nostalgiacollection.com

Printed and bound in Great Britain

The publishers are grateful to Tony Wright and Philip J. Kelley for their help with photographs for this new edition. Drawings are by the author unless otherwise credited.

**Title spread Great Western country: a scene on the famous Pendon layout.** *Tony Wright, courtesy British Railway Modelling*

A Silver Link book
from
*The* NOSTALGIA *Collection*

# PREFACE

This book was first published in 1990 and received much acclaim as a concise guide for those aspiring to model the Great Western Railway or its successor, British Railways Western Region, and was endorsed by no less an authority than the Great Western Society, Didcot, as 'an invaluable guide to modelling this much loved company, and a fine potted history as well'.

In the intervening 12 years much has changed, not least the continued development of exciting new models, particularly ready-to-run in OO gauge, and there has been a rapid growth in the interest and consequently the number of products for O gauge. Neither could be anticipated back in 1990. The continuing growth of detailed treatises on the Great Western and the republishing of books long out of print demonstrate that interest in the GWR shows little sign of diminishing, yet, as time gets the better of us all, the numbers who remember the steam era, let alone the GWR, must sadly continue to decline.

We therefore thought at Silver Link that it was time the book re-appeared, so the editorial team has updated the text and pictures from the original PSL publication, but it remains largely as written back in 1990. We hope you find it a useful 'ready reference' to the Great Western and its successor.

# CONTENTS

Timber viaducts were a characteristic feature of the GWR in the West Country. Here 'Star' 4-6-0 No 2927 *Saint Patrick* crosses Treviscoe Viaduct on Chris and Steve Knight's OO gauge layout. *Tony Wright, courtesy British Railway Modelling*

# INTRODUCTION

The Great Western Railway, arguably the most popular of Britain's major railway companies, inspires to this day, more than 50 years after its demise, tremendous support from enthusiasts, preservationists, and railway modellers. It has also been comprehensively documented, from detailed locomotive histories to its company servants and individual and insignificant branch lines.

We hope that we can bring objectivity to this guide and provide, as much as one can ever hope to in one slim volume, the information necessary to enable anyone interested to model a basic GWR layout. Clearly, as interest develops, then more specialist and detailed knowledge can be sought and acquired. To this end a Select Bibliography is given in Appendix 1.

The prime interest in the GWR seems to be in the 1930s. The content of this book inevitably reflects this, but it would be remiss not to mention the Broad Gauge era and the individuality of Brunel's GWR. Similarly, this individuality continued on the Western Region of the nationalised British Railways, so due coverage is also given to reflect the growing interest in modelling the post-nationalisation period.

We hope that those embarking for the first time on the enjoyable and absorbing task of building a model railway based on the Great Western or its successor will find the book useful and encouraging, and that those whose knowledge of the GWR and whose modelling experience is greater may also find something of interest in the ensuing pages.

A scene familiar from countless 'real-life' photographs: the curve on to the sea wall at Teignmouth, Devon, here faithfully recreated on the Pendon layout. *Tony Wright, courtesy British Railway Modelling*

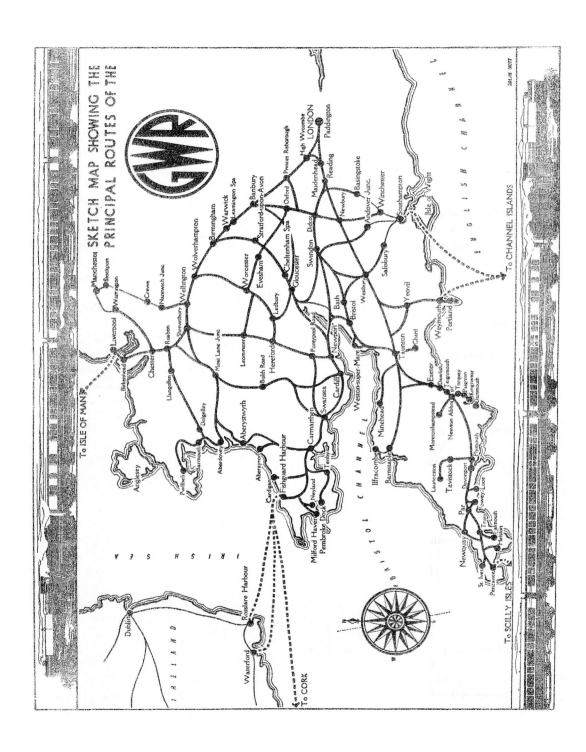

# 1
# THE GREAT WESTERN RAILWAY

'**D**ear old Great Western! Line of great expresses and paralysed locals! Pompous, gas lit, loveable old humbug!' So wrote C. Hamilton-Ellis in *Four Main Lines* (George Allen and Unwin, 1950).

God's Wonderful Railway or Gas Works Railway, loathe it or love it, you can't ignore the Great Western Railway. How much of the legend is due to the nostalgia of holiday journeys to the West Country by GWR or Western Region, and how much to the very adroit Publicity Department, prominent in the 1930s, we will never know. But the latter must take significant credit. In its heyday before the Second World War it produced jigsaws, books and all manner of publicity material, including some excellent films, to celebrate its achievements and recreate past glories, such as the relaying of 171 miles of broad gauge track in the West Country in 1892. It is even said that, much to the disgust of the CME, the Publicity Department insisted on having streamlined locomotives so that the company wasn't seen to be falling behind the LNER and LMS, which in the late 1930s were stealing a march in publicity with their streamlined 'A4' and 'Coronation' 'Pacific' locomotives. Thus the rather peculiar bullet smokebox, 'V'-fronted cab and fairings were produced for a 'Castle' and 'King' Class loco.

Never missing a publicity opportunity, the centenary of the Royal Assent for the Bill for the Great Western Railway in 1935 was adroitly chosen by the company as the year to celebrate its first 100 years, rather than the date of opening of the first stretch of line; this action thus pre-empted any centenary celebrations the LMS may have planned in 1937 to commemorate the opening of the Grand Junction Railway.

So what was the Great Western Railway? Everyone knows it had green engines with copper-capped chimneys, 'chocolate and cream' coaches and holiday expresses to Devon and Cornwall with evocative names like the 'Cornish Riviera Express'. In this first chapter we will take a broad look at the Great Western Railway and how it developed, to set the scene for subsequent chapters that deal with specific areas such as locomotives and signalling.

## The formative years

The origins of the Great Western Railway lie in a meeting of business and civic leaders in Bristol in January 1833 to discuss the making of a railway from London to Bristol. A young engineer, one Isambard Kingdom Brunel, was chosen as Engineer, and thus the Great Western Railway, then still the Bristol & London Railroad, was ensured of its character, idiosyncrasies and all.

The Bill for the Great Western Railway received the Royal Assent in August 1835, the line from London to Bristol opening on 30 June 1841. Brunel was already well established as an engineer, having submitted the winning design for the Clifton Suspension Bridge in Bristol. He brought his individual style to the railway from the beginning, architecturally with his 'roadside' and 'chalet' styles of station building, but most importantly by choosing the 'broad' gauge of 7ft 0¼in for the railway itself. Not only was the broad gauge unusual, but its construction with rails supported on continuous longitudinal timbers – the 'baulk road' – caused much controversy at the time.

Branches were laid from Didcot to Oxford, and Swindon to Gloucester. A mixed gauge line

What was the Great Western Railway? For many it was the charm of its rural branch lines, and these prove perennial favourites with modellers. This is Vic Halliwell's 'Hallbury' in EM scale. *Tony Wright*

from Oxford to Birmingham via Banbury was opened in 1852, connecting the GWR with the West Midlands and, ultimately, North and Central Wales and Birkenhead. A broad gauge South Wales Railway was sponsored from Gloucester to Cardiff, Swansea and Carmarthen, to tap into the vast South Wales coal and mineral traffic potential. Ultimately it was hoped to provide a short sea route to Ireland. The South Devon line reached Plymouth in 1849. Brunel experimented with atmospheric traction between Exeter and Newton Abbot, but it was a short-lived experiment of 18 months or so. The Cornwall Railway continued the broad gauge to Truro, where the standard gauge (4ft 8½in) West Cornwall was met, the latter eventually selling out to the Cornwall Railway, which was then able to complete the broad gauge line to Penzance, the Royal Albert Bridge over the Tamar at Saltash providing another example of Brunel's genius.

The spread of Brunel's broad gauge met with increasing opposition from standard gauge companies over the inconvenience of changes in gauge. Eventually the Government set up a Gauge Commission, and subsequently a Royal Commission recommended that the broad gauge should not be perpetuated. The GWR decided to abandon it in 1891, culminating in the now famous conversion of 171 miles of track between Exeter and Truro in a weekend, a feat reconstructed for a famous film by the GWR publicity machine in the 1930s. The last broad gauge train left Paddington on 20 May 1892, ending an era, but not the individuality of the Great Western Railway.

The GWR continued its expansion and development in the latter half of the 19th century, forging ahead to Yeovil, Taunton and, via a mixed gauge line, to Weymouth, from where ferry services to Cherbourg were introduced between 1878 and 1885. In 1889 the GWR took over the Channel Island ferry service from Weymouth, an altogether more successful venture.

Continuing to extend its empire and influence, it not only built its own extensions and new lines, but also acquired other smaller

Modelling the GWR in the Broad Gauge era is less common, but here is a charming scene on Bob Harper's 'Teign-house Sidings'. Note the early Brunellian 'disc and crossbar' signal (see page 99). *Tony Wright, courtesy British Railway Modelling*

railways and ran others that were nominally independent. Routes were improved and several more direct lines built. The Severn Tunnel was opened in 1886; at 4 miles 628 yards long it is still the longest tunnel in Britain. Its construction took 13 years and seemingly stretched the company's resources almost to the limit. However, it reduced the distance between Paddington and Newport by 15 miles and was typical of the spirit with which the company pursued route improvements in the period up to the 'Grouping' of Britain's railways in 1923.

The GWR was at one time nicknamed the 'Great Way Round' because many of its routes were somewhat less than direct. Its original main line had, of course, reflected its birthright, the Bristol to London route. This made many subsequent routes awkward, not least those to South Wales, which the Severn Tunnel improved. Consequently there were a whole series of new routes and improvements made in the first years of the 20th century, to such an extent that by the outbreak of the First World War the railway was scarcely recognisable as the GWR of the 19th century. New 'cut-off' routes included Birmingham to Stratford-upon-Avon, Honeybourne to Cheltenham, Taunton to Castle Cary, Westbury to Putney, Paddington to High Wycombe, and Princes Risborough to Banbury.

New routes, new carriages and faster trains combined to provide competitive services, not least with the LNWR to Birmingham with the introduction of 2-hour trains between that city and Paddington.

# The Grouping

The Great Western Railway was the least affected of all the companies when Britain's myriad railway companies were 'grouped' into the 'Big Four' in 1923. The majority of the 26 subsidiary companies that became part of the GWR group had been operated by the larger company for many years and had already been subsumed into the GWR system.

Officially constituents rather than subsidiaries under the terms of the Railway Act of 1921 were six other companies, all operating in Wales. These are worthy of brief comment as kits are

available for some of the locomotives and items of rolling-stock that these companies ran, and these could be seen for many years after the Grouping alongside standard GWR locomotives and stock, albeit in the case of the locomotives often modified with standard GWR features. For the sake of completeness, all six are mentioned, although they vary considerably in significance.

### Alexandra (Newport & South Wales) Docks & Railway

This railway's principal mileage was in docks and sidings, 100 miles compared to 9 miles of open line, the latter forming part of a route from Pontypridd to Newport over which a passenger service ran, taken over by the GWR in 1899. In later years the route was extended to Machen over the Brecon & Merthyr line and was worked by steam railmotors. The company had its own locomotives, including two 2-6-2 Hawthorn Leslie tank locos of 1920, both of which were still in service at nationalisation.

### Barry Railway

The Barry Railway was planned as a combined railway and dock system, providing an outlet for coal, particularly from the Rhondda. It provided a new dock at Barry, with running powers over the Taff Vale and a passenger service from Barry to Porth. Similar arrangements with the Great Western provided access to Cardiff. There was a branch line from Barry to Barry Island, which provided significant passenger traffic to what was a very popular resort.

Despite the association of the South Wales railways with coal traffic, the Barry Railway did have its own named passenger express train, 'The Ilfracombe Boat Express', which ran non-stop from Cardiff to Barry in summer to connect with the company's own steamer service across the Bristol Channel. It also participated in working the 'Port to Port' Cardiff-Newcastle express of the Great Western, Great Central and North Eastern railways, the Barry Railway providing the locomotive power for the Cardiff-Barry section of the journey in the halcyon days before the First World War. The Barry Railway had a number of locomotives and items of rolling-stock for which kits are available.

## Cambrian Railways

The Cambrian was unique amongst the Welsh railways, first because it sprawled across the remoter parts of Central and West Wales, a true cross-country railway, and second because it operated the narrow gauge Vale of Rheidol Railway and was closely involved with the affairs of a second narrow gauge system, though of a different gauge, the Welshpool & Llanfair.

The Cambrian ran from Oswestry and Whitchurch to Aberystwyth, west to Pwllheli and south to join the Brecon & Merthyr at Talyllyn Junction near Brecon. It connected with the Great Western at Oswestry and with the GWR & LNWR Joint line from Shrewsbury at Buttington.

The former Cambrian system has been a popular source of inspiration for the model railway builder, perhaps because of its association with holidays or the delightful locomotives that it operated, such as the Sharp Stewart 2-4-0 tanks of the Tanat Valley section or the 'Dean Goods' and 'Manors' of later years. There are suitable models of locomotives associated with the Cambrian available in both kit form and ready-to-run for 4mm scale.

## Cardiff Railway

The Cardiff Railway originated as yet another attempt to provide transport from the mines of the valleys to the docks. Despite its plans, only one short line was built linking the Rhymney Railway at Heath Junction outside Cardiff to the Taff Vale at Treforest. The junction with the latter was the subject of prolonged litigation and was eventually dismantled; a 450-foot viaduct over the River Taff was left unused and subsequently demolished, the line terminating at the Cardiff side of the river.

A loaded coal train from the valleys to the South Wales docks behind '42XX' Class 2-8-0T No 4247 runs through Sully station on the former Taff Vale Railway, modelled in OO by the Barry & Penarth Model Railway Club. *Tony Wright*

## Rhymney Railway

This was again built to provide a link between the mineral deposits of a Welsh valley, the Rhymney, with the town of the same name and the Bristol Channel. There was a direct line from Caerphilly to Cardiff and a joint line with the LNWR from Rhymney to Nantybwch, connecting via the LNWR line to Abergavenny. There were also running powers over other lines and a joint route with the GWR to Merthyr via Aberfan.

In the golden era of railway travel before the First World War, the railway carried through coaches over the LNWR via Abergavenny to Liverpool and Manchester. Like so many other similar facilities these were withdrawn during the Great War, never to return.

Several kits for locomotives and coaching stock of Rhymney Railway prototypes have been available.

## Taff Vale Railway

Probably better known to students of law, social history and politics as a result of a strike in 1906 and the implications of subsequent legislation, the Taff Vale Railway operated well over 100 route miles. It formed a network of lines in the Cardiff area and a harbour was constructed at Penarth. Its principal traffic was coal, but it was an early user of railmotors on local branch line passenger services.

A few kits of Taff Vale Railway locomotives have been manufactured, the most notable being the South Eastern Finecast white metal body kit for a 4mm scale 'U1' Class. A Taff Vale 'O2' Class tank has been restored to its original condition on the Keighley & Worth Valley Railway after NCB modification.

The Great Western Railway inherited a diverse collection of locomotives and stock from these South Wales railways. Many of the locomotives survived for a long period under the GWR, some being 'Swindonised' in the process. If the South Wales railways can be said to have contributed anything to Swindon locomotive matters, then surely it must be the development of the 0-6-2T. This was developed into almost a South Wales type, not gaining much favour elsewhere in the country, but being found ideal for coal and mineral traffic in the valleys. The Collett '56XX' owes its development to South Wales practice, and indeed the majority of these GWR engines spent their lives in Wales.

On the coaching side, ex-Barry Railway coaches were still in use on the Culm Valley line in Devon in the 1950s.

That then was the Great Western Railway from the early days to the Grouping. It was very much business as usual for the GWR after 1923, the Grouping causing little outward change, except in South Wales. The basic foundations to take the Great Western forward to nationalisation had already been laid, and in all the departments of the railway developments were along those well-established lines, rather than any radical change.

The ensuing chapters deal with the aspects of the GWR likely to be of interest to the modeller. Those interested in the company history of the GWR; its hierarchy and organisation are referred to those publications listed in the Bibliography.

# 2
# LOCOMOTIVES

There are more models of GWR locomotives, both in ready-to-run and kit form, than of any other company in 4mm scale, and significant coverage in N and O gauge, although currently no ready-to-run models exist in the latter. There is, however, a ready-to-run Class 121 'bubble car' in O gauge, ideal for diesel-era branch and local services.

In addition to the ever-changing range of ready-to-run models and kits, a staggering range of components is available, particularly in 4mm scale, to convert and detail ready-to-run models. Although adding to the cost of the model, they do provide a relatively straightforward way of obtaining an accurate and varied collection of GWR locomotives.

In this chapter we will take a look, in brief, at locomotive development on the GWR and Western Region of BR, including a description of engine classification, power groups and route colours. Details are also given of some of the particular features or modelling difficulties to be borne in mind if effective models are to be made.

The Great Western Railway was unique in having all its main-line locomotives developed by itself to suit its own requirements. There was also a direct lineage of association between the men in charge of locomotive affairs: Churchward had worked under Dean, Collett under Churchward, and Hawksworth first under Churchward and subsequently Collett. While the traditions established were maintained, each subsequent CME built on and developed these principles. It has, however, been argued that such continuity led ultimately to stagnation.

## Locomotive development

### Broad gauge beginnings

Between 1837 and 1854 the entire locomotive stock of the GWR was broad gauge. Although Brunel was generally responsible for the design of the earliest locomotives, it appears that such activities were not his forte, and Daniel Gooch took over as Locomotive Superintendent in 1837.

Motive power made a less than auspicious start on the GWR. Brunel ordered initially a variety of locomotives from outside contractors; *North Star*, from Robert Stephenson & Co of Newcastle, seems to have been the most successful of these very early locomotives, and this 2-2-2 type was perpetuated, as was a larger-boilered version.

The first locomotive built at Swindon was a version with 8-foot-diameter driving wheels; it was ultimately given a leading bogie, thus becoming a 4-2-2 and the basis of the 'Iron Duke' Class, of *Lord of the Isles* fame. In these formative years, true GWR broad gauge locomotives were not numbered, but were identified only by name. The broad gauge locomotive situation can best be summarised by reference to the accompanying table.

The first standard gauge locomotives in GWR stock were those of the Shrewsbury & Chester and Shrewsbury & Birmingham railways, which became part of the GWR in September 1854. Swindon turned out its first standard gauge loco in May 1855, No 57, an 0-6-0 goods engine. New locomotives were built at Wolverhampton in 1859, 2-2-2s being the first. No new locomotives were built there after 1908, all new construction thereafter being concentrated at Swindon, although occasionally outside contractors were used.

*Left North Star*, the first locomotive to run on Brunel's broad gauge. This non-working replica was produced for the company's centenary in 1935, the original having been scrapped in 1906. *BR*

*Right Lightning*, a 4-2-2 of the 'Iron Duke' Class. *BR*

*Below Stromboli*, one of the 0-6-0T broad gauge locomotives sold to the South Devon Railway that later returned to GWR stock in 1876 when the SDR was acquired. Then numbered 2138, it is seen modelled in Scale 7 on Bob Harper's 'Teignhouse Sidings'. Note the characteristic broad gauge goods wagons glimpsed under the overall roof. *Tony Wright, courtesy British Railway Modelling*

## Table 1: GWR broad gauge locomotives

| Class or type[1] | Wheel arrangement[2] | Number built | Class or type[1] | Wheel arrangement[2] | Number built |
|---|---|---|---|---|---|
| 'Star' | 2-2-2 | 12 | 'Premier' | 0-6-0 | 12 |
| 'Firefly' | 2-2-2 | 62 | *Bacchus* | 0-6-0 | 1 |
| 'Sun' | 2-2-2 | 21 | 'Pyracmon' | 0-6-0 | 6 |
| 'Prince' | 2-2-2 | 6 | 'Caesar' | 0-6-0 | 8 |
| Not classed | 2-2-2 | 18 | 'Ariadne' | 0-6-0 | 26 |
| *Great Western* | 4-2-2[3] | 1 | 'Caliph' | 0-6-0 | 76 |
| *Thunderer* | 4-2-2 | 1 | 'Swindon'[7] | 0-6-0 | 14 |
| 'Iron Duke' | 4-2-2 | 29 | 'Metropolitan'[8] | 2-4-0T | 22 |
| 'Iron Duke'[4] | 4-2-2 | 24 | 'Corsair' | 4-4-0T | 2 |
| 'Leo' | 2-4-0[5] | 18 | 'Sappho' | 4-4-0T | 13 |
| 'Victoria' | 2-4-0 | 18 | 'Banking'[9] | 0-6-0T | 5 |
| 'Hawthorn' | 2-4-0[6] | 26 | 'Sir Watkin'[9] | 0-6-0T | 6 |
| 'Waverley' | 4-4-0 | 10 | | | |
| 'Hercules' | 0-6-0 | 4 | **Total broad gauge engines built[10]** | | **441** |

1 Some class names changed *circa* 1865 and certain engines differed in detail while nominally of the same class.

2 Some 2-2-2s were later altered to 2-2-2T and 4-2-2T.

3 *Great Western* was originally built as a 2-2-2.

4 Replacements of the original 'Iron Duke' Class.

5 All became 2-4-0Ts.

6 10 of the class became 2-4-0Ts.

7 All sold to the Bristol & Exeter Railway, returning to GWR stock in 1876 as Nos 2077-90.

8 Originally condensing locomotives; seven were converted to 2-4-0 tender locos.

9 One of the 'Banking' and three of the 'Sir Watkin' classes were sold to the South Devon Railway. They later became GWR stock again as Nos 2138 and 2157-9 in 1876, when the SDR was acquired.

10 No purely broad gauge locos were built after 1866, but a large number of 'convertible' engines were.

Two standard gauge locomotives from the Dean era: a superb 7mm model of 'River' Class No 70 *Dart* scratch-built by Tony Reynalds, and the very famous 'City' Class 4-4-0 No 3440 *City of Truro*, now part of the National Collection. *Tony Wright/Ray Ruffell, Silver Link collection*

## The Churchward era

Churchward's major policy contribution was to implement a policy of standardisation of components, aiming for the common use of as many parts as possible in a variety of locomotive types. There remained, however, considerable numbers of Armstrong and Dean types at the Grouping.

Churchward's first task was to produce six-coupled express passenger locomotives. The taper boiler was adopted from American practice and De Glehn compounds purchased from France to evaluate compounding. Ultimately the 'Saint' Class 4-6-0 was developed from these experiments and the scene was set for the development of the 'Stars', 'Castles' and 'Kings'.

A range of five standard boilers was developed, the first, the No 1 boiler, being used in the 'Stars' and 'Saints'. The standard driving wheel diameter was 6ft 8½in for these express passenger 4-6-0s until the 'Kings' were developed, which had 6ft 6in driving wheels.

Three 'one offs' were designed by Churchward, which never became standard types. The 'County' Class 4-4-0s and the equivalent tank engines, the 4-4-2 'County' tanks, were built in comparatively small numbers and utilised the Swindon No 2 boiler. There was also the one-off 'Pacific', *The Great Bear*.

Churchward's '45XX' Class was, surprisingly, not considered a standard class, having few major components that were interchangeable. He developed the '42XX' 2-8-0Ts for the South Wales coal traffic, and this class was perpetuated under Collett. The '43XX' 2-6-0s for mixed traffic use were also perpetuated after the Grouping with minor modifications and a new design of cab.

Churchward also continued to build earlier designs of 0-6-0 tank locomotives, modifying many. The GWR was a considerable user of saddle tanks and later pannier tanks. Large numbers of the latter were built as replacements for earlier locos to a standard design by Collett, Churchward's successor, from 1922. Thus the archetypal GWR loco arrived on the scene. A variety of types were developed between the '57XX' Class of 1929 and the taper boiler '94XX' tanks of 1948, including the series of 11 '97XX' condensing locomotives for use over the Metropolitan lines in the London area on both passenger and freight traffic. There were two other post-war developments of the ubiquitous pannier tank. One was the '16XX' Class, one of which, No 1646, worked the Dornoch branch in Scotland. The second was the '15XX' Class, very American in appearance with outside cylinders and valve gear, taper boiler and no running plate as such.

Churchward's pioneering 4-6-0: a Mitchell 4mm 'Star', No 4004 *Morning Star*, built by Mike Edge and painted by Ian Rathbone. *Tony Wright*

*This page* 2-6-2T Prairie tanks of the Churchward era. The Modelex '44XX' 'small Prairie' is an O gauge model built by Chris Dunne, while the later '45XX', No 5570, photographed in 1958 at Dovey Junction, has larger tanks with tapering fronts. Finally '61XX' No 6126 is larger again and intended for suburban passenger work; photographed at Oxford at 1965, it has just worked a special train. *Tony Wright, courtesy Pat Ryan (Modelex)/Ray Ruffell, Silver Link collection (2)*

*Opposite page* '57XX' 0-6-0 pannier tank No 7713 in prototype and model form, the former photographed at Minehead in 1960. Note that the O gauge model version is fitted with a spark-arresting chimney, and is seen at the coaling stage on Terry Yeend's 'Tolcarn Engine Shed' layout, based on Chippenham. *Ray Ruffell, Silver Link collection/Tony Wright*

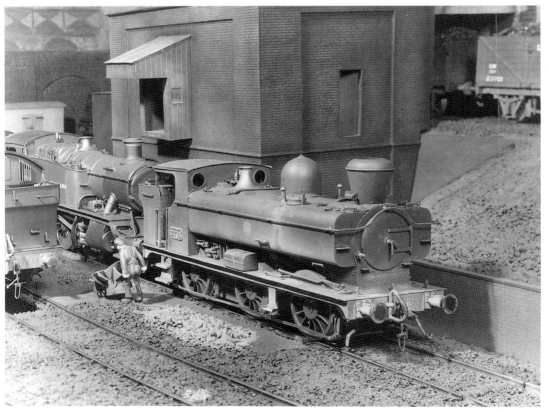

Another beautifully detailed O gauge '57XX' pannier, built by Eric Harrison from a Vulcan kit. *Tony Wright*

A slightly later '64XX' pannier tank on a typical working at Merthyr in 1961, having worked in from Pontsticill Junction. *Ray Ruffell, Silver Link collection*

## The Collett era

Collett's first task on taking over as CME in 1922 was to produce a new express locomotive to take advantage of the greater axle load permitted by the Civil Engineer's Department. The result was the four-cylinder 'Castle' Class 4-6-0, a continuation of Churchward's principles, developed from the 'Stars' but with unmistakable Collett characteristics, such as the side-window cab. The design was so successful that it was perpetuated after nationalisation, the last batch being built in 1956.

The 'Kings' were the next development, and the last express 4-6-0 on the GWR, incorporating the largest boiler built by Swindon and with a curious front bogie with the leading wheels carried in outside-frame axleboxes, the rear with inside-frame axleboxes. This curiosity, an unmistakable characteristic of the 'Kings', resulted from the reluctance to depart from the Churchward principle of cylinders having horizontal centre lines, which gave a clearance problem in the new locos.

The 'Hall' Class was developed from the 'Saints' when *Saint Martin* was rebuilt with smaller 6-foot-diameter driving wheels. Ultimately 330 of these practical, mixed traffic locos were built.

The 'Grange' Class, with smaller 5ft 8in driving wheels, appeared in 1936, ostensibly to provide a fast service for produce trains from the West Country, Cornish broccoli in particular, and fruit from other areas to the London markets.

A Collett curiosity appeared in 1936 with the rebuilding of the 'Dukes' and 'Bulldogs'; it was actually a combination of 'Bulldog' frames and 'Duke' boilers, producing what were officially known as 'Earls' but colloquially became 'Dukedogs'. These were lightweight locomotives with outside frames, which were useful on the heavily restricted Cambrian lines until wartime improvements enabled more modern and heavier locomotives to be used. Amazingly it is rumoured that, for once, the Publicity Department failed and many of the titled personages after whom the locos were named were less than amused at being associated with such antiquated engines!

The final pre-Second World War 4-6-0, the 'Manor' Class, appeared in 1938, a small two-cylinder loco with 5ft 8in driving wheels.

The 0-4-2 tank had been an important design in the early days, the Wolverhampton-built Armstrong '517' Class being particularly useful on branch line and light suburban passenger duties. Collett set about replacing this venerable and much modified class and introduced the '48XX' and '58XX' 0-4-2 tanks. The former were push-pull fitted and totalled 75; the latter were not so fitted, and numbered 20. They were introduced in 1932 and built until 1936. Eventually, in 1946, the '48XX' Class assumed the better-known numbering series of 14XX. They remained largely unaltered save for the addition of top feeds from 1948.

Collett's '2251' Class of 0-6-0s is also worthy of mention, being particularly useful to the modeller. These locomotives were introduced in 1930, perpetuated until the last batch was built between 1944 and 1948, and were to be found all over the system and even, after nationalisation, on the Somerset & Dorset line. They were a continuation of the classic British loco design, the 0-6-0 tender engine, maids of all work, and were intended to replace the by then rather ancient Dean type on the main lines, leaving these lighter though older machines free for use on the Cambrian. In fact, the last of the 'Dean Goods' was not withdrawn until 1957.

An O gauge 'Castle' 4-6-0, No 5006 *Tregenna Castle*, on the evocatively named 'Holiday Haunts' layout by Michael Price, John Porter and Mike Heaven. *Tony Wright*

We three 'Kings'... No 6010 *King Charles I* is a Jamieson 4mm model by David Amias; No 6013 *King Henry VIII* is a South Eastern Finecast (ex-Wills) P4 model running on 'Aberhafren'; and the close-up of the O gauge model of No 6021 *King Richard II* (built by Malcolm Mitchell and painted by Alan Brackenborough) shows a wealth of magnificent detail, as well as the characteristic front bogie of the 'Kings'. *All Tony Wright; No 6021 courtesy Pete Waterman*

*Top and middle* Mixed traffic: 'Hall' 4-6-0 No 4954 *Plaish Hall* of 1929 on station pilot duties at Banbury in 1957, and preserved 1949 BR-built 'Modified Hall' No 6998 *Burton Agnes Hall* on display at Didcot in 1975. *Both Ray Ruffell, Silver Link collection*

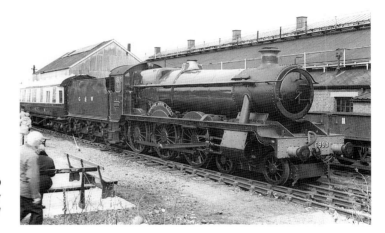

*Below* O gauge 'Grange' Class 4-6-0 No 6836 *Estevarney Grange*, built by Dave Murdoch. *Tony Wright, courtesy British Railway Modelling*

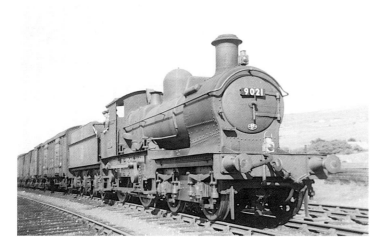

*Top and middle* Collett's 'Dukedog' 4-4-0s worked mainly on the Cambrian lines. Here No 9021 heads an afternoon freight at Llwyngwril, south of Barmouth, in 1958. Sister loco No 9016 is seen in O gauge model form from a Gladiator kit. *Ray Ruffell, Silver Link Collection/Tony Wright, courtesy Pete Waterman*

*Bottom* No 7816 *Frilsham Manor* in O gauge model form, built by Lee Marsh and painted by Alan Brackenborough. *Tony Wright, courtesy Pete Waterman*

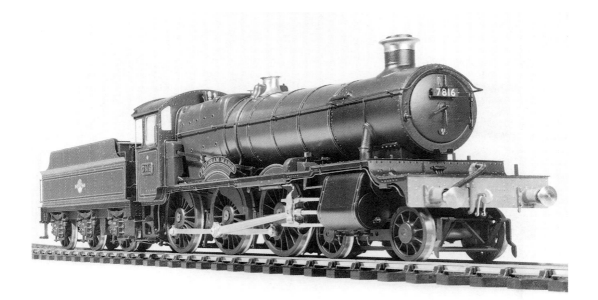

When introduced in 1932 Collett's push-pull-fitted 0-4-2 tank locos were known as the '48XX' Class. Versatile branch line locos, 'auto-tank' No 4807 is seen on Ken Cottle's 'Weston Green' Scale 7 layout. They later assumed the better-known 14XX number series; No 1419 is seen propelling its auto-train at Fowey in 1957. *Tony Wright/Ray Ruffell, Silver Link collection*

The versatile Collett '2251' Class were to be found all over the system and eventually even on the Somerset & Dorset line. No 3216 was photographed at Highbridge in 1961 on the 2.20pm to Evercreech Junction. *Ray Ruffell, Silver Link Collection*

## Hawksworth developments

F. W. Hawksworth, the final CME of the GWR, took office in 1941 and despite the adversities of wartime conditions, economic difficulties and the trauma of nationalisation, brought some useful designs to the stock.

Most prominent was the 4-6-0 'County' Class, the final two-cylinder 4-6-0 type to be developed, introduced in 1943. Most noticeably, these locomotives departed from earlier appearances by the use of continuous splashers above the footplate and large slab-sided tenders.

Hawksworth introduced the 'Modified Hall Class' in 1944. The locomotives had a plate-frame bogie with a wheelbase 2 inches longer, and are most distinguishable by the frame extension over the front footplate, which arose from the batch having plate-frames carrying the buffer beams, rather than the Churchward bar frame extension; in Churchward's designs the main frames ended at the rear of the cylinders.

The last two types of pannier tank, the '15XX'

and '16XX' Classes already mentioned, were attributable to Hawksworth.

## Freight locomotives

Before leaving this necessarily broad outline of GWR locomotive development, mention of the principal freight locomotives would not go amiss.

Two large tank locomotives were developed by Churchward for South Wales coal traffic. These were the 2-8-0Ts of the '42XX' series and the 2-8-2Ts of the '72XX' series. The latter were essentially a larger-bunkered variation of the former to enable long-distance working; in fact, the 54 locomotives of this class were rebuilt '42XXs'. Although the majority of the '42XX' Class were employed in South Wales, two were shedded for many years at St Blazey, Cornwall, for china clay traffic to Fowey. The '42XX' locos include several variations of which the modeller should be aware: originally they had straight frames, then drop frames with a raised portion

'28XX' 2-8-0 No 3863 of 1903 on a railtour at Swindon in 1965. Primarily a freight loco, they could occasionally turn up on regular passenger workings. *Ray Ruffell, Silver Link collection*

over the cylinders and outside steam pipes; various boiler fittings were also used.

Churchward designed two large freight locos, both 2-8-0s, the '28XX' and '47XX' Classes. The former were perpetuated by Collett and later batches featured his side-window cab and drop frames; there were eventually 166 of these locos. Initially for coal traffic, they graduated to general heavy freight use and could often be seen on summer Saturday relief trains. They lasted until 1964, although withdrawal had started two years earlier. The '47XX' series was Churchward's last design and appeared 16 years after the first '28XX' in 1919. They had 5ft 8in diameter wheels as opposed to the 4ft 7in of the '28XXs', and were intended for fast night freights, but were found to be useful mixed traffic locos and, like the '28XXs', could be seen on relief trains. Only nine were built.

The Collett '56XX' tank is worth mentioning, being the Great Western's answer to the popular South Wales 0-6-2T for coal traffic; 150 were built, and though many never strayed from South Wales, they could be seen in small numbers all over the system except the West Country. They were often used for passenger duties.

The GCR Robinson-designed 2-8-0s were built in large numbers for the Railway Operating Division (ROD) of the Royal Engineers during the First World War, then after the war the Government encouraged their purchase by various railways, although in the absence of vacuum brakes they were only suitable for unfitted freight. The GWR initially purchased 20 locos and, after hiring 84, bought a further 80 when the Government reduced their price. The GWR converted 50, adding top feeds, superheaters, copper fireboxes and other standard features, while the remaining 50 were scrapped, the last in 1931. The converted locos lasted well, the last, No 3036, going in 1958. The 50 scrapped locos did not take their tenders with them, and these were put to use most frequently behind the 'Aberdare' Class. Specific mention is made of these locomotives because they seem popular with GWR modellers and there has been an acceptable kit available in 4mm scale.

*Opposite page* Two of only nine '47XX' 2-8-0s built, seen in prototype and model form. No 4702 poses for an official photographer, while sister loco No 4703 emerges on to the seawall in the O gauge 'Holiday Haunts' layout. *BR/Tony Wright*

*Top and middle* '56XX' 0-6-2T No 6652, during and after work to mount its Bachmann body on a replacement Comet chassis. *Both Tony Wright*

*Right* 0-6-2T No 6682 on its home ground at Cardiff Queen Street with a train from Rhymney in 1961. *Ray Ruffell, Silver Link collection*

An ROD 2-8-0 as purchased and converted by the GWR. This is a Little Engines model in OO. *Tony Wright*

## British Railways developments

Locomotive development on the Western Region of British Railways deserves a brief word, not only because of the already mentioned perpetuation of various steam locomotive types, but also because of the unique pattern of developments under 'dieselisation' when steam on the Western Region ended in 1965.

The first point to establish is that the GWR itself experimented with diesel traction, not only with its well-known railcars but also with a small 70hp Fowler 0-4-0 shunter and 350hp English Electric-powered diesel-electric shunters. However, save for two gas-turbine/electric locomotives, one from the Swiss firm of Brown-Boveri, the second from Metropolitan-Vickers, there were no further flirtations with this form of traction until after the British Transport Commission produced its Modernisation Plan.

Politics now enter the scene, which is beyond the scope of this book. Suffice to say that nationally diesel-electric was the favoured traction, whereas the Western Region, because of the nature of its routes, in particular the heavily curved and graded lines of the West Country, favoured lighter but high-performance diesel-hydraulics based on the successful Deutche-Bundesbahn V200 locomotives.

The typical British compromise resulted in the Western Region having its diesel-hydraulics, but an insistence on their being British-built resulted in the North British Locomotive Company's 'Warships' (later Class 43), which

provided a locomotive considerably heavier than was wanted. Subsequently a lighterweight version, which became the Class 42, was built, a more successful locomotive in keeping with the Western Region's original requirements. The West of England was the first area of the Western Region to be dieselised, the Class 43s taking over the 'Cornish Riviera Express' in June 1958.

The North British Bo-Bos of the D63XX series (later Class 22), also diesel-hydraulics, were introduced in 1958, followed the following year by the Beyer-Peacock 'Hymeks' (Class 35), which proved very successful. The 'Western' diesel-hydraulics (Class 52) were introduced in 1961, proving to be powerful locomotives and improving long-distance express times; 74 were built in all.

The end for the diesel-hydraulics was in sight, however; in 1963 diesel-electric locos began to appear. Large numbers of Brush Type 4s (Class 47) were introduced over the next two years, and English Electric Type 3s (Class 37) were used in pairs on the fastest expresses. 'Peaks' (Class 45s)

*Above right* Days of transition: a '47XX' 2-8-0 heads a Class C fitted freight (note the headlamp code – see Appendix 4) and is overtaken by a North British 'Warship'. The scene is Sonning Cutting, modelled in OO by Steve and Chris Knight. *Tony Wright, courtesy British Railway Modelling*

*Right* Western Region diesel-hydraulics pass at 'Oxendale Junction', Wolverhampton MRC's N gauge layout. The locomotives are D1000 *Western Enterprise* and 'Hymek' No D7007. *Tony Wright, courtesy Irwell Press*

D1030 *Western Musketeer* at Exeter St David's with a down express in 1966. It sports BR blue livery, and the first coach is an ex-LNER standard Thompson TK – a useful precedent for modellers who might like to mix their Regions! *Tony Wright*

hauled through trains from other regions, as did English Electric Type 1s (Class 20) on freights. Electrification elsewhere saw the release of further diesel-electrics, and in 1968 the first 'Warships' were withdrawn, the original series all going during that year, the rest having gone by 1972. Brush Type 2s (Class 31) arrived on the Western in 1969, followed in 1972 by other Type 2s of Class 25. The 'Hymeks' had gone by 1975, and the 'Westerns' gradually disappeared between 1973 and 1977. Class 50s were displaced by the electrification of the West Coast Main Line to Glasgow, and by 1976 all of the class had been sent to the Western. The Southern Region Class 33 could also later be seen regularly on Western metals, in particular in the West Country.

So much for the main-line express locomotives, but what about the more mundane services more appropriate to the small model railway? Railcars were seen as the saviour of rural branch lines and various types were tried on the Western, in addition to those that the GWR had

built itself. The AC four-wheel railbus is probably the best known of these and a kit is available in 4mm scale. These were used on, among others, the Tetbury branch; five were built and each provided 46 2nd Class seats. Later the larger Class 121 and 122 railcars were introduced and saw service during the last years of passenger workings on many West Country branch lines that hung on into the early 1960s.

Pressed Steel Class 117 and Derby 116 three-car units are part of the large fleet of DMUs used on the Western Region. There were also three-car Gloucester Carriage & Wagon suburban sets. The Swindon cross-country sets are also notable, having a large headlight for working the Central and West Wales lines. These ran in both two-car and three-car sets over these routes. Single-car motor parcels vans, following on from the GWR type, were also allocated to the Western.

The Class 142 DMUs, a combined Leyland Bus/BR development utilising bus bodies on rail chassis, were introduced in 1987 for local trains. In the West Country they were known as 'Skippers'.

One of the Western Region's Gloucester RC&W Co motor parcels vans, No W55991, a direct descendent of the GWR's railcars, on the Cardiff (Whitchurch) Model Engineering Society's 'Whitchurch Road' OO layout. *Tony Wright*

Two further DMUs are noteworthy. The first, the Metro-Cammell 'Blue Pullman' trains, ran between Paddington and Birmingham, Bristol and latterly South Wales. Secondly, the HSTs, or Intercity 125s, have revolutionised journey times and passenger comfort on the Region's main express services.

This brief resumé is not intended to be more than an outline of locomotive changes on the GWR and its successor. The reader's attention is directed to Appendix 1, which provides sources of further information, some of which is very detailed and will provide all the information a modeller is likely to require.

# Numbering and power classification system

### The numbering system
Fortunately, the GWR, unlike many of its contemporaries, showed a reluctance to renumber locomotives. It is therefore a comparatively straightforward task to trace

particular locomotives and identify them by class and number. However, throughout the years to the Grouping, the continued expansion of the GWR involved the acquisition of other railway companies. This in turn brought to the GWR a variety of locomotives, some of which it had sold to those companies and were thus returned to GWR stock. This, together with the addition of new locomotives of its own, led to several attempts at renumbering, culminating in a major scheme in 1912, the main purpose of which was to tidy up the allocation of numbers generally. Moreover, the 1912 scheme laid the foundations of the class numbering system adopted by the company, in which the second of the four figures of an engine's number was intended to relate to a particular wheel type. For example, the 40XX, 50XX, 60XX and 70XX series were all four-cylinder 4-6-0s; 29XX, 39XX, 49XX, 59XX, 69XX and 79XX were two-cylinder 4-6-0s; 31XX, 41XX, 51XX, 61XX and 81XX were large-wheeled 2-6-2Ts; and so on.

All prototype engines and other standard

designs with odd numbers were brought into line by being included in the number series of later examples, and future series of locomotives were to be numbered from 0 to 99. There were various consequential alterations; for example, small-wheeled 2-6-2Ts Nos 3101-10 were altered to the 4401-10 series so that all large-wheeled 2-6-2Ts could be in the 31XX series.

There were of course later alterations to this planned sequence when the two-cylinder 'County' Class 4-6-0s were numbered in the 10XX series, and the 68XX and 78XX series were used for the small-wheeled 'Grange' and 'Manor' Classes. The 48XX 0-4-2Ts were later renumbered in the 14XX series to allow the 2-8-0s to be included in the 48XX series.

The 1923 Grouping brought the greatest influx of stock to the company, and obviously renumbering into the standard GWR system was a major task. In the main this was accomplished by adding the acquisitions into number series between 1 and 1390, which at that time were vacant. The Grouping brought back into the fold many standard locomotives that had been sold to the companies amalgamated into the GWR, and these assumed their original GWR numbers. All locomotives renumbered at this time bore the letters 'GWR' above the numbers on the number plate, including this latter category of acquisitions.

## Engine classification, power groups and route colours

From 1920 Great Western locomotives were grouped into seven classifications based on tractive effort, and these were shown on the cabside above the number plate by a letter on a coloured disc. The coloured disc indicated the weight restriction of that locomotive.

The power classification was represented by the following letter code:

| Power class letter | Tractive effort (lb) |
| --- | --- |
| Ungrouped | Below 16,000 |
| A | 16,500-18,500 |
| B | 18,501-20,500 |
| C | 20,501-25,000 |
| D | 25,001-33,000 |
| E | 33,001-38,000 |
| Special | Over 38,000 |

The weight restrictions/route availability were in five categories, represented, as already mentioned, by coloured discs displayed above the cabside number plate. They were as follows:

| Route colour | Axle load |
| --- | --- |
| Uncoloured | Up to 14 tons |
| Yellow | Up to 16 tons |
| Blue | Up to 17 tons 12 cwt |
| Red | All engines over 17 tons 12 cwt except the 'King' Class |
| Double Red | 22 tons 10 cwt ('King' Class) |

There were additional restrictions; for instance, red engines could not exceed 20mph on dotted red routes, nor blue engines exceed 25mph on dotted blue routes. Prior to the Second World War the 'Kings' were only able to work over the following routes: Paddington to Devonport via Newbury and Bristol; Wootton Bassett to Bristol via Badminton; and Paddington to Wolverhampton via Bicester. From 1948 the 'Kings' were permitted between Bristol, Pontypool Road, Shrewsbury and Wolverhampton.

The Second World War caused some revision of route classification, usually as a result of engineering works; for instance, the Cambrian line from Oswestry to Aberystwyth was upgraded from yellow to blue. The '57XX' locos, which had a blue restriction, were reclassified yellow by BR.

It is worth also mentioning that in the war years, other companies' locomotives working over the GWR had route colours and power groups allocated to them, as follows:

| Company | Class | Route colour | Power class |
| --- | --- | --- | --- |
| SR | S15 | Red | D |
| SR | N15X | Red | C |
| LMS | 8F | Blue | E |
| LNER | O4 | Blue | D |
| WD | 'Austerity' 2-8-0 | Blue | E |
| LNER | V5 | Yellow | A |
| SR | I3 | Red | C |

Certain other locomotives, notably 'County', 'Hall', 'Grange' and ex-ROD 2-8-0s were permitted, during the war, to haul loads in excess of those designated. This was indicated on the cabside by the addition of a white 'X' painted above the cabside plate. This practice continued for some time after the war, but whether it was officially sanctioned after nationalisation we have been unable to verify.

Finally, by way of an example, the following list sets out power classes and route restrictions of GWR locomotives still in service on the Western Region of BR in the early 1960s:

| Class | Route restriction | Power class |
|---|---|---|
| 'County' | Red | D |
| 'Castle' | Red | D |
| 'Hall' | Red | D |
| 'King' | Double Red | Special |
| 'Grange' | Red | D |
| 'Modified Hall' | Red | D |
| 'Manor' | Blue | D |
| '28XX' | Blue | E |
| '45XX' | Yellow | C |
| '5101' | Blue | D |
| '61XX' | Blue | D |
| '81XX' | Blue | D |
| 56XX' | Red | D |

| Class | Route restriction | Power class |
|---|---|---|
| '1361' | - | - |
| '1366' | - | - |
| '15XX' | Red | C |
| '47XX' | Red | D |
| '43XX' | Blue | D |
| '2251' | Yellow | B |
| '72XX' | Red | E |
| '42XX' | Red | E |
| '14XX' | - | - |
| '16XX' | - | A |
| '54XX' | Yellow | - |
| '57XX' | Yellow | C |
| '97XX' | Blue | C |
| '64XX' | Yellow | A |
| '74XX' | Yellow | A |
| '94XX' | Red | C |

The above notes are included because they indicate quite clearly the restrictions on the use of locomotives at various periods and will help the more fastidious modeller to avoid the possibilities of using unsuitable locomotives on his model railway.

# 3
# COACHING STOCK

The subject of Great Western coaching stock is both lengthy and complex. Coaches are, however, essential to the majority of model railway layouts, and some knowledge of them is necessary to enable their realistic use on the model if an authentic GWR or Western Region scene is to be portrayed.

There are a number of excellent books giving histories of the subject, to which those wanting detailed information, perhaps to model a specific vehicle, are referred. Two publications spring particularly to mind as providing all the information the modeller is likely to need: *Great Western Coaches* by Michael Harris (David and Charles, latest edition 1985) and Jim Russell's excellent series *Great Western Coaches*, Vols 1 and 2, and *Great Western Coaches Appendix*, Vols 1 and 2, (OPC, 1972-3). This chapter, therefore, will give just a brief outline of major developments, styles and types of coaching stock. The illustrations show far more clearly than words some of the particular idiosyncrasies of design and most of the particular characteristics of Great Western style.

The number of models available and the continual introduction of new ones and withdrawal of others makes a definitive list impossible to compile; keeping a watchful eye on the model press and at trade stands at major exhibitions is the best means of keeping abreast of developments and availability.

The outline starts at around 1890, at a time when the first corridor stock to be built for a British railway was introduced by the Great Western (the doors were kept locked, however, to prevent passengers moving about the train!).

## Coaching development

### The pre-Churchward era
The 1890-91 corridor stock entered traffic the following year on the Paddington-Birkenhead service, and in doing so created a precedent for the future of express stock on British Railways by introducing the through corridor with connections between vehicles. This train was the first to have connections between all vehicles, and had a side corridor and accommodation for 1st, 2nd and 3rd Class passengers. The coaches were clerestory roofed, similar in style to other vehicles of the period. There was a communication cord for emergency use, a hotel-style bell call to the guard, and steam heating. The connecting doors between carriages were, however, kept locked, the guard having the key. The gangway connections were a natural continuation of the line of the side corridor and were therefore at the side of the coach end, making the vehicle, as it were, 'handed'. As the use of corridor vehicles spread, additions to these trains were difficult to make if the corridor connection was to be maintained, leading to the gangway being moved to a central position. The vehicles were withdrawn in the early 1930s.

Convertible coaches, that is vehicles with broad gauge bogies but narrow bodies, anticipating the end of the broad gauge with the minimum of rebuilding, were still being built in 1890. Coaches of the period were of the familiar Dean clerestory type, which over the years, and despite the variety of vehicles built, changed little. The bogies were of an overall similarity, only the wheelbase varying; these early Dean bogies appeared in 6ft 4in, 8ft 6in and 10ft wheelbases. The common types used on the Great Western are shown in Figure 1 to enable modellers to identify the types referred to.

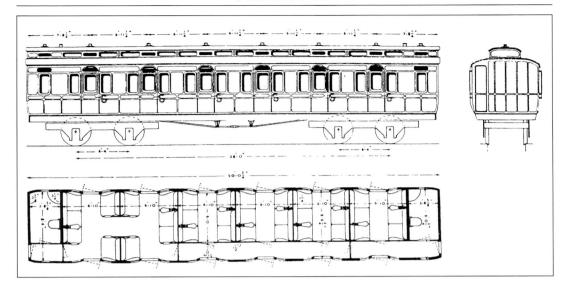

*Above*  A GWR drawing of a 1st Class carriage from the GWR's first corridor train of 1891-2. Note the side corridor and off-centre connecting door in the coach end.

*Below*  Figure 1: Rough outlines of the principal four-wheel bogies used by the GWR.

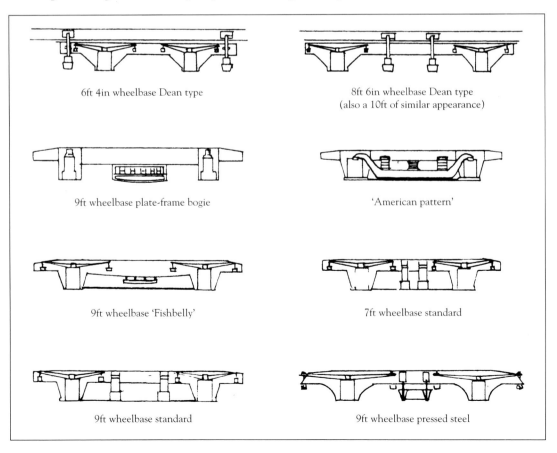

6ft 4in wheelbase Dean type

8ft 6in wheelbase Dean type
(also a 10ft of similar appearance)

9ft wheelbase plate-frame bogie

'American pattern'

9ft wheelbase 'Fishbelly'

7ft wheelbase standard

9ft wheelbase standard

9ft wheelbase pressed steel

Most trains of the late 1890s were still non-corridor, except for the crack expresses. Through coach working over branch lines and on other companies' systems was usually catered for by Brake Tri-composite corridor vehicles.

Further corridor sets were introduced in 1893, for the prestigious 'Cornishman' service, the first train to run non-stop through Swindon, all trains hitherto having been required to stop there to enable passengers to use the refreshment rooms as a result of a curious agreement between the GWR and the proprietors of the facility stemming from the earliest days of the company. Similar vehicles were also later introduced on South Wales services. These vehicles returned to the use of quarter-lights in the corridor side windows rather than the large single bay windows of earlier cars. They had separate ladies' and gentlemen's toilets, clearly reflecting social attitudes of the day, and ran on Dean standard 8ft 6in bogies. The 'Cornishman' train comprised six vehicles with a Tri-composite Brake added in the summer timetable for conveyance over the Newquay branch.

These vehicles really set the style for the archetypal Dean clerestory vehicles built over the next ten years or so. They suffered the same problems with the gangway position as the earlier Birkenhead sets, but as the sets were broken and vehicles replaced, they were similarly modified to facilitate general use. Some were later converted to electric lighting, and in 1905 one was converted to the unique auto-coach No 14. All but a few of the vehicles had been withdrawn by the end of the last war, withdrawal having commenced in the early 1930s.

A feature of Victorian and Edwardian rail travel was the ability to hire various saloons for private use. All the railway companies had family and invalid saloons during this period. The family saloons were quite luxurious and, for those who could afford their hire, private transport and accommodation, these vehicles were almost a home from home, being 1st Class and, in some instances, even providing a luggage compartment and accommodation for servants. There were also less luxurious vehicles for the other classes.

Where there were suitably located railway lines, many of the major social and sporting events of the day attracted considerable numbers of saloons, which acted as a base for their hirers during the event. These coaches were predominately of the six-wheel types, but four-wheel examples were built and, later, bogie types. Indeed, one four-wheeled example continued in its intended use until 1923; it was then converted for use as a fruit van, in which form it lasted until 1933. Ten clerestory-roofed, six-wheel saloons were built at this period, four 1st Class saloons and six family saloons that included servants' accommodation. Eight-wheel vehicles began to appear in 1892, initially a 38ft 6in family saloon, but later vehicles, including a 56-foot Directors Saloon, were considerably larger. There were also contemporary saloons used on the Royal Train as required.

By 1890 four-wheel general service passenger coaches were built principally for branch lines or other specific use, such as suburban services. Some 600 four-wheel vehicles were built between 1890 and 1902, 200 of which, designed for London suburban services, were of reduced height and width with short buffers, except at the ends of the sets where they were of normal length. The vehicles in these sets were rebuilt with conventional buffers when the sets were broken up and the vehicles dispersed in the 1920s. By the 1930s four-wheel vehicles had been relegated to service on the more remote and less important branch lines or for workman's trains, particularly in South Wales. The Highworth branch was one line still utilising four-wheelers at this time, and the Burry Port & Gwendraeth was another, until the end of passenger services in 1953. Some vehicles were converted into camping coaches and a great many ended their days in departmental use.

The 1892 corridor train and its successors, particularly on the West of England services, were very successful, and from the mid-1890s the production of corridor stock increased rapidly. Corridor coaches of this period were of a fairly standard design, which continued until 1904. The difference in the vehicles, apart from their types, was principally length (various lengths were built between 50 and 58 feet), internal layout, clerestory side detail and window styles.

A variety of three-centre-roofed, non-corridor

A Ratio four-wheel coach in use on Rex Ashton's P4 'Llwynmawr'. By the 1930s such vehicles had been relegated to service on the more remote and less important branch lines or for workmen's trains, particularly in South Wales. *Tony Wright, courtesy British Railway Modelling*

vehicles were produced between 1895 and 1898 for branch line use, former broad-gauge frames and bogies being used on some vehicles. Six- and seven-compartment Brake 3rds were built in 1895 and used for suburban services, while 15 Tri-composite Brake coaches were produced specifically for branch line service. Some of these vehicles were later formed into 'B' sets (see below), and three-coach sets of 51-foot vehicles were formed for specific services. All had gone by 1950.

In 1902 a 68-foot clerestory Brake 3rd was built and heralded as the shape of things to come, being the precursor for the construction of subsequent 70-foot-long vehicles. It was withdrawn in 1950 after many years in use as the famous 'whitewash coach', used for testing the riding of various bogie designs.

A small batch of 69-foot elliptical-roof Brake Composites was introduced in 1905. Retaining much external similarity with earlier vehicles, but without the clerestory roof, they lasted into the 1950s, little changed save for the removal of guard's duckets on some.

### The Churchward era

Churchward not only revolutionised locomotive matters on the Great Western but also coaching stock design. His first vehicles were truly massive, 70 feet long and 9ft 6in wide, built to take full advantage of the generous clearance and loading gauge afforded the Great Western as a result of its broad gauge beginnings. They had elliptical roofs and sounded the death knell of the clerestory. These massive coaches earned the name 'Dreadnoughts', a direct comparison to the ever-larger battleships being built at the time by Britain in the arms race with Germany.

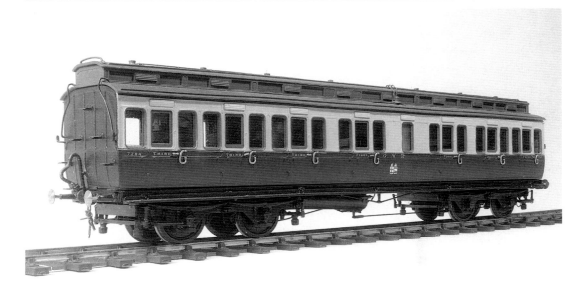

*Above*   An finely detailed O gauge clerestory coach by Ian Rathbone. *Tony Wright*

*Below*   Detail of an O gauge Churchward 'Dreadnought' coach, painted by Ian Rathbone. *Tony Wright*

'Toplight' vehicles from PC kits on the P4 'Dartley' layout. *Tony Wright*

The first 'Dreadnought' vehicles were the restaurant cars of 1904, which initially ran in sets made up of clerestory-roofed stock. Ordinary stock at first comprised three seven-car sets for the Paddington-Penzance 'Cornish Riviera Express'. The coaches were, however, not popular on these services and were replaced on the 'Cornish Riviera' in 1914. The coaches had another distinguishing feature other than their size. There were no external doors to the compartments, entry and exit to the vehicles being by end and central vestibules, which had recessed doors. The corridors changed from one side of the vehicle to the other on either side of the central vestibule. These vehicles had quite a long life, the last going in 1956, having declined in prestige to post-war stopping trains and relief sets.

Further 70-foot stock was built in 1906 and was, once more, to alter radically the appearance of coaching stock on the Great Western Railway. The new vehicles provided more accommodation and, to allow the maximum width of 9 feet overall, had their doors inset. This gave rise to their curious appearance and their nickname of 'Concertina' stock. The 9-foot extreme width allowed the vehicles over more routes, in particular in South Wales. They had toplights above the windows, a feature to be perpetuated in the next style. 'Concertina' restaurant cars and slip coaches also appeared, but they all went in the 1950s.

The most characteristic of the pre-Collett era carriages were built in considerable numbers between 1907 and 1920, in a variety of lengths, 56 feet, 57 feet and 60 feet. These coaches were easily distinguishable by the oblong hammered glass lights above the quarter-lights and full lights, which gave them their common nomenclature of 'Toplight'. They had full panelling above the waist and appeared in various types, the 56-foot and 57-foot versions of which are sometimes referred to and identified by reference to Bar 1, Bar 2 or Multibar, which related to their underframe bracing, but also corresponded to variations in body panels and mouldings. 70-foot 'Toplight' stock was also produced in significant numbers for prestigious express use, whereas the short vehicles were intended for lesser services. Apart from those

sold to the Government for use as ambulance trains during the First World War, the 'Toplights' lasted well, a few even into the early 1960s. The 'Toplight' style was utilised on a variety of vehicles, including Full Brakes, CCTs, special saloons, sleeping cars and restaurant cars.

### The Collett era

Further changes in style occurred with new stock introduced in 1923, with the start of the use of bow-ends to vehicles. The first vehicles were 70 feet long and formed two sets of seven coaches each, including a restaurant car that had both 1st and 3rd Class accommodation. The composites and restaurant car had bow-ends, Pullman-type gangways and buckeye couplings. The 3rd Class vehicles had bow-ends and buckeye couplings at one end only, the other end being square with standard couplings. This was to enable other standard coaches to be inserted to strengthen the set, should that be necessary. Normal buffers were fitted to the coaches, but at the ends where the buckeye couplings were fitted they were arranged to hinge down when the buckeyes were in use. The buckeye couplings were removed in 1934. These were the last 70-foot vehicles to be built.

Non-corridor 'Toplight' stock was also produced during this era in 48-foot and 60-foot lengths, the last appearing in 1922. The non-corridor varieties, however, appeared in limited numbers in comparison with corridor vehicles. American and later lightweight bogies were used on the 'Toplights'.

The year 1923 saw the introduction of 57-foot bow-ended corridor stock, which continued in production until 1929. These vehicles followed the style established with the refurbishment of earlier 70-foot vehicles on which the bodies had been modernised with steel panels. The first vehicles had elliptical roofs and flat ends running on 9-foot bogies. From 1925, bow-ends and 7-foot bogies became the standard for general service vehicles. Originally some vehicles were marshalled into six-car sets and eight-car all-3rd excursion sets were also formed. Restaurant and sleeping cars were also built in this style. The vehicles lasted well, the last being withdrawn in the 1960s. Indeed, one ex-buffet car is at the time of writing still in use as an inspection saloon.

Non-corridor stock to a similar design was built in large quantities with, again, the earliest being flat-ended and running on 9-foot bogies. Some were marshalled into permanent four-coach sets for suburban duties, others into two-coach 'B' sets. The 'B' sets comprised of two close-coupled brake composites and were intended as permanent formations for branch line and other stopping services. These 'B' sets were used into the early 1960s, many being allocated to the Bristol area, while some West Country branches also benefited from them. Table 2 lists vehicle types and numbers that were formed into 'B' sets.

The Great Western Railway, like other companies, experimented with articulated stock, and corridor and non-corridor restaurant and kitchen cars were produced. This stock was converted to normal bogie types in the 1930s, except for the suburban types, which finished

### Table 2: GWR 'B' sets

| Diagram No | Date built | Running numbers | Dimensions | Comments |
|---|---|---|---|---|
| E.116 | 1924 | 7169/70, 7171/2, 7510/1, 7574/5, 7576/7, 7578/9, 7625/6 | 57ft 0in x 9ft 0in | |
| E.129 | 1926 | 6545/7, 6551/3, 6556/60, 6561/3, 6565/6 | 58ft 2in x 9ft 0in | For Bristol Division |
| E.135 | 1929 | 6640/1, 6642/3 | 58ft 2in x 8ft 10¼in | For Bristol Division |
| E.140 | 1930 | 6445/6, 6447/8, 6449/50, 6451/2, 6453/4, 6455/6, 6457/9, 6460/1, 6462/3, 6464/5 | 61ft 2in x 9ft 3in | For Bristol Area |
| E.140 | 1930 | 6381/2, 6409/10, 6411/2, 6413/4, 6470/1, 6523/4, 6534/5, 6537/8, 6541/2, 6548/9, 6589/9, 6703/4, 6722/3, 6894/5, 6979/80, 6986/7, 6995/6, 6999/7000 | 61ft 2in x 9ft 3in | |
| E.140 | 1931 | 6240/1, 6261/2, 6365/6, 6371/2, 6374/5, 6656/7, 6968/9, 6975/6, 6977/8, 6983/4, 6989/90 | 61ft 2in x 9ft 3in | For Bristol Division |
| E.145 | 1933 | 6061/75, 6122/23/59/61/68/75, 6180/86/88/91/93/99, 6200/02/04, 6215-17/19-22/24/25/28/29/32/ 34/38/39/46/51/53/54/57/63/68/97, 6316/35/38/48/59/61/63/67/68/73 | 61ft 2in x 9ft 3in | |
| E.147 | 1933 | 6762/3, 6764/5, 6769/70, 6771/2, 6773/4, 6776/7, 6778/9, 6781/2, 6783/4, 6785/6, 6787/8, 6789/90, 6791/2, 6793/4, 6796/7, 6800/1 | 57ft 0in x 9ft 0in | For Newport Division |
| E.147 | 1934 | 6873-6/78-85/87-91/93/96-9/ 6900-04/6906-08 | 57ft 0in x 9ft 0in | |
| E.147 | 1935 | 6803, 6813-5, 6817/9/21 | 57ft 0in x 9ft 0in | For Newport Division |
| E.147 | 1936 | 6711/15/25/26/27/28/30/32/36/38/ 39/40/41/43/45/46/48/49/51/53/ 55/56/58/59/60/67/98/99 | 57ft 0in x 9ft 0in | |

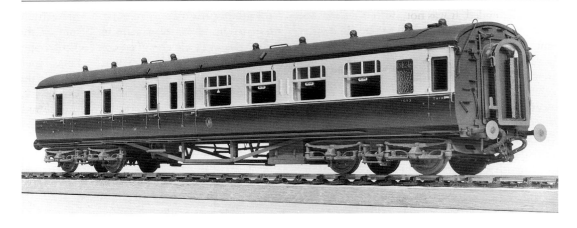

*Above*   Rodney and Vera Cooper's prize-winning Collett coach in P4, based on a Comet kit. *Tony Wright*

*Below*   A GWR drawing of a Collett 1st/3rd Composite 'Centenary' corridor coach of the 1930s.

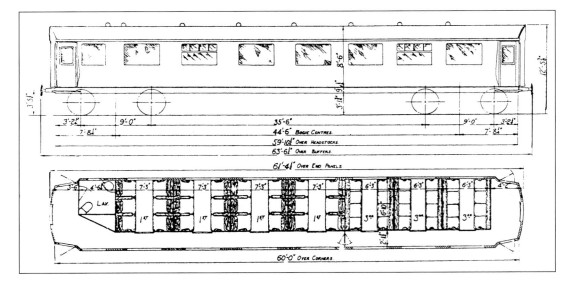

their days in original condition. This stock was found usually on London suburban services and in Bristol and South Wales.

The 1929-33 period saw the introduction of flush-sided, flush-window corridor stock, 60 feet long and running on 9-foot-wheelbase bogies. This stock was first introduced on the 'Cornish Riviera', Torbay and other West of England expresses, and matching dining and kitchen cars were also produced. These were wide-bodied vehicles, 9ft 7in, which somewhat restricted their use, a fact that was denoted by a red triangle painted on each end of the vehicle. Similarly styled vehicles, but only 9ft 3in wide,

were introduced for general use in the early 1930s, and 9-foot-wide versions followed for cross-country lines and use over other companies' systems. Sixty-foot suburban coaches to the same outline also appeared, some being marshalled into sets. Pairs of brake composites coupled together again formed 'B' sets but had short buffers on the inner ends. These vehicles, like earlier 'B' sets, saw much branch line service.

### The Hawksworth era

The impending end of the Second World War led to plans being laid for new stock well before hostilities ended. It was not, however, until well after the war that any new stock appeared, immediate post-war economic conditions precluding the developments optimistically planned for, not only within the railway industry but also generally.

Hawksworth's carriages brought a new shape to Great Western coaches. They had straight, flat sides without a tumblehome, sloping or drop-ended roofs, which made them easily distinguishable, and continued the use of large windows and low waists of immediate pre-war designs. The Hawksworth stock had 64-foot body lengths and 9-foot bogies, and the first of these corridor vehicles entered service in 1946. The introduction of these coaches saw the beginning of a new post-war livery for coaches on the Great Western; they also broke away from earlier trends in that they did not immediately go to form crack West Country expresses. Indeed, the only sets into which these vehicles were made up were for Birmingham-West Country and Birkenhead-Bournemouth services, the vast majority of the Hawksworth corridor stock being used loosely and often on stopping and branch line services.

These were the last Great Western-designed corridor coaches to be built, and the fact that they were not used in sets on the principal expresses foretold the future, as by 1956 all main-line expresses on the Western Region were composed of the new standard BR Mk1 stock. The Hawksworth corridor coaches lasted until 1968 and a few even managed to receive the blue/grey BR livery.

Significant quantities of non-corridor suburban stock began to appear in 1950. This stock bore the same overall design features as the Hawksworth corridor coaches, being flat-sided with flat ends and a long 63-foot body but without the drop-ended roof; these coaches ran on 9-foot bogies. Five 'B' sets were formed from Brake Composites for use in the Plymouth area.

The introduction of DMUs on suburban and local services, and the closure of branch lines, meant that this stock was to have a very limited life. In fact, the end came quite quickly with the announcement by BR Western Region of the end of all non-corridor stock by the close of 1963.

There were two other types of vehicle designed in the Hawksworth style. The first, the only special vehicles to be built to this shape, were four 64-foot 1st Class sleeping cars, which lasted in service until 1970. The second were the 24 auto-coaches built to replace ageing vehicles then in use, many of which were still the rebuilds of original steam railmotors. These latest auto-coaches were very much in the body style of other contemporary vehicles already mentioned but without the sloping end roof. The first two vehicles, Nos 220 and 221, were named 'Wren' and 'Thrush'. Fortunately this naming was not perpetuated on the rest of the vehicles. These two worked in the London area, the remainder principally in the Gloucester area.

# Special vehicles and slip coaches

The main types of special coaching stock vehicles included restaurant cars, kitchen and sleeping cars and luggage and passenger brake vans.

Restaurant, kitchen and sleeping coaches were built in the majority of styles of coaching stock and have been mentioned earlier in passing; these vehicles are, however, not very relevant to the average modeller. Slip coaches, on the other hand, may well be of more interest, and a brief outline of their operation and development is given below, while the various 'brown' vehicles are outlined in Chapter 6.

As regards luggage and passenger brake vans, a variety of vehicles in styles similar to contemporary coaching stock were built from the earliest days to provide space for the conveyance of luggage and parcels, accommodation for a guard and appropriate braking facilities. These vehicles, being of a similar style to and moving in passenger trains, usually carried appropriate passenger coach liveries.

The first vehicles of this nature built for the standard gauge were of a four-wheeled design. Various types were built, in lengths between 28 and 31 feet. However, the majority of the early examples were 40-foot-long bogie vehicles, bearing the external features of standard Dean coaching stock but with three-centre roofs rather than clerestories and running on 8ft 6in bogies. Later vehicles were longer; two distinct batches were built, one of 46ft 6in vehicles and another of 48ft 6in. The shorter vehicles were predominantly used for the conveyance of newspapers. The later batches of these vehicles had gangway connections and American bogies. Vehicles of this type had a long life, and although many ended their days in departmental use, often as store vans, they were still running in their intended use in the 1940s.

Seventy-foot 'Dreadnought' vans were constructed, together with many other special vehicles for Atlantic liner traffic. These Ocean Mails vans are mentioned because after the First World War they were displaced on this prestige duty and were used in ordinary service as newspaper vans.

Passenger brake vans, often referred to as Full Brakes, were also built in the 'Toplight' style in significant numbers in both 56ft 11in and 57ft lengths, and ran on the same 9-foot American equalised bogies as the ordinary 'Toplight' coaches. The 57-foot vehicles had wooden body panelling and mouldings, the others steel panelling. These two varieties were long-lived vehicles, lasting in general service until 1962.

The bow-ended style from the mid-1920s also produced vehicles that were still in service in 1962. These vehicles originally replaced the 'Dreadnoughts' on the Ocean Mails service, but later, with the demise of this service, were put to more mundane general service duties. They ran on the then new 7-foot bogies, as did the later 61-foot vehicles.

Passenger brake vans 57 feet long with 9-foot bogies were introduced in the mid-1930s, in two body widths, some with side corridors in the same style as ordinary coaches of the period. The last built before the Second World War were of 59-foot length. Many of these vehicles were still in service in the early 1970s, by then, of course, in BR blue.

The post-war Hawksworth designs also spawned 45 64-foot passenger brake vans, the last of which did not disappear until 1979.

## Slip coaches

The Great Western was well known for its use of slip coaches. Slipping was the practice of releasing coaches from moving trains to enable stations to be served without through trains having to stop. The first slip coach service was introduced in 1858, the last surviving until 1960. Slip coaches were not connected by gangways to the remainder of the train and indeed, at the beginning, not even the steam heating was connected. However, this latter deficiency was remedied in 1908 and the former problem was solved temporarily by including a restaurant car in the four-coach slip portion of the 'Torbay Express' prior to the last war. Four coaches was the maximum number allowed to be slipped, and 70-foot vehicles were barred from slipping. The number of slip services steadily dwindled after the First World War, though small numbers continued to be built, including some post-Second World War conversions of Hawksworth corridor stock.

# 4

# Railmotors, auto-trains and diesel railcars

It is convenient to consider railmotors, auto-trains and diesel railcars at the same time because they were each intended to provide effective and efficient solutions to lightly patronised services either as supplements to peak loco haulage or, as in the case of diesel railcars, to speed up services in competition to the increasing inroads being made by road transport. The auto-trains were a much more versatile answer, enabling loads to be varied quite considerably and easily in response to passenger demand and with a much greater ability to tow non-passenger vehicles, perhaps in response to a seasonal peak in perishable produce.

These three forms of rail transport are in themselves interesting but have found a particular niche amongst railway modellers, where they provide an ideal and relatively easy answer to providing realistic short passenger services on small-space model railways. The Great Western used them to such an extent that they have become almost the archetypal image of that company's extensive branch line network.

The same aims that pushed the Great Western into using these vehicles also prompted its constituent companies in South Wales to use steam railmotors and auto-trains, the former in quite large numbers proportionately. The earliest use of steam railmotors, however, goes back to the Bristol & Exeter Railway in the late 1840s. Much later, in the late 1930s, streamlined diesel railcars became a well-known aspect of Great Western operations. However, the first internal combustion passenger-carrying vehicle used by the GWR was in 1911, when a petrol-electric railcar was used.

This chapter is divided into three sections dealing with each type of conveyance, giving a brief outline of the development of the vehicles

and of the types of locomotive used for auto-train working. The popularity of these vehicles with modellers has ensured that some excellent kits and ready-to-run vehicles have been produced in the popular scales.

## Steam railmotors

Among the railways participating in the railmotor boom of the early years of the 20th century, the GWR was a giant, operating by far the largest fleet of steam railmotors for longer than anyone else.

The origins of steam railmotor usage lie with the trial of Drummond's joint LB&SCR/LSWR car, designed for the Fratton-Havant line. The Great Western introduced its own design of railmotor later in 1903 on the Chalford-Stonehouse line. New halts were built – a feature discussed in Chapter 7 – which at first encouraged railmotor usage by developing more traffic but, as happened later with diesel railcars, later led to the downfall of such vehicles as traffic increased beyond their ability to handle it.

The first steam railmotors, Nos 1 and 2, in some ways anticipated some of the features of later 'Dreadnought' stock. They differed from contemporary coach design, having high elliptical roofs and large windows with big, pull-in ventilators at the top. They were slab-sided and flat-ended, had matchboarding below the waist and were 57 feet long and 8ft 6in wide. All later railmotors were bow-ended.

Twelve more, Nos 3 to 14, were constructed the following year, 59ft 6in long, together with two matching trailers, one 59ft 6in long, the other 70 feet long. Further batches, Nos 17 to 28, were also constructed in 1904 for use in the London area. There were several detail variations in these early cars, the principal ones for the modeller to be aware of being the varying driving wheel diameters employed, the initial two having 3ft 6in wheels, whereas 4-foot-diameter wheels were used from No 37 onwards. Two peculiarities among the railcars were Nos 15 and 16, which were built by Kerr Stuart and Co to that company's design. No 15 was sold to the Nidd Valley Light Railway, and No 16 was finally withdrawn in 1927.

Railmotors were classified as 'branch' or 'suburban' types, which referred to whether the vehicles had luggage accommodation or not. The branch line type had this facility, while the suburban type occupied this space with seats.

Further railmotors were built to continue the expansion of steam railmotor services. Nos 29 to 36 were of branch line type, and were 59ft 6in vehicles. Nos 37-40 were 70 feet long, while 41 and 42 reverted to 59ft 6in. Nos 43-52 were again 70-foot vehicles, as were Nos 53-60. This series of railmotors was of a different style, having bowed ends and sides curving in at the bottom. They had bolection moulding around the windows and frosted glass toplights. The 70-foot vehicles had the interior divided into two saloons, and there was a central entrance vestibule and retractable steps. There were various detail differences between vehicles in this sequence and some were intended to work as two-car sets with a trailer.

Trailers appeared to various designs, the majority being 70-foot vehicles. While there

| Table 3: Steam railmotor construction | | | |
|---|---|---|---|
| Diagram No | Date built | Running Nos | Dimensions (ft in) |
| A/A1 | 1903 | 1-2 | 57 0¼ x 8 6¼ |
| B/C/D | 1904 | 3-14 | 59 6¼ x 8 6 |
| F/G/G1 | 1904 | 17-28 | 59 6 x 8 6 |
| H/J/J1 | 1905 | 29-36 | 59 6 x 9 0 |
| K/K1 | | 37-40 | 70 0 x 9 0 |
| L | 1905 | 41-2 | 59 6 x 9 0 |
| M/M1/N | 1905 | 43-52 | 70 0 x 9 0 |
| O | 1905 | 53-8 | 70 0 x 9 0 |
| P | 1905 | 59-60 | 70 0 x 9 0 |
| E | 1905 | 15-16 | 56 3¾ x 9 0 |
| O | 1906 | 61-72 | 70 0 x 9 0 |
| Q | 1906 | 73-80 | 59 6 x 9 0 |
| Q1 | 1907 | 81-3 | 59 6 x 9 0 |
| R | 1908 | 84-90 | 70 0 x 9 0 |
| R | 1908 | 91-9 | 70 0 x 9 0 |

were differences amongst them, No 48 was quite unique. This car had centrally located seating and an open gangway at either side, an attempt to overcome some of the problems of access and egress. Seventeen railmotors were still in service up to 1935, and full details of the duties that these vehicles undertook are contained in the RCTS's *Locomotives of the GWR*, Part 13. Modellers should note that the railmotors always carried the stopping passenger headlamp code.

A GWR drawing of a 59ft 6in suburban-type steam railmotor.

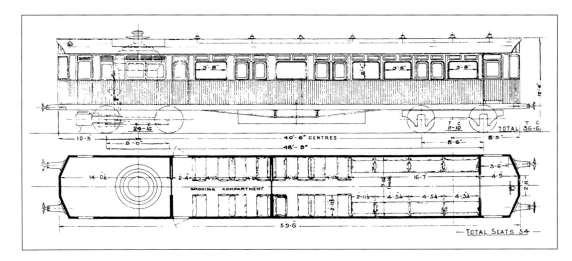

# Auto-trains

Despite the fact that the Great Western Railway pursued railmotor use and design to a greater extent than any other British railway, the problems of haulage capacity and versatility were insurmountable. The railmotors had been successful in their originally envisaged use of supplementing short-distance services and working all passenger services on quieter branch lines where the use of trailers was not required. However, the inherent problems of self-propelled vehicles, in particular their lack of flexibility and limited power, was their downfall. They had developed business beyond their capabilities in several instances, which had led to peak services having to revert to locomotive-hauled trains.

In 1905, experiments began in the Plymouth area with the use of a '517' Class 0-4-2 tank sandwiched between a pair of two-car trailer sets similar to those used with the railmotors. The locomotive was equipped with manual control gear enabling the train to be operated from the outer ends of the trailers. The experiment was obviously successful and the age of the auto-train had arrived. Various locomotives were auto-fitted, though originally it fell to smaller, older types to carry out these duties.

Until the advent of the '14XX' Class, the principal types so used were the '517' Class, the Metro 2-4-0T and '2021' Class with 4ft 1in driving wheels. Undoubtedly examples of other classes were also used in this way. There were various oddities, such as the fitting of a few auto-train locos with a coach-body-type 'casing' for a short period before the First World War.

Auto-train services were accelerated at the beginning of the 1930s and, after experiments with pannier tank No 2080 fitted with 5-foot diameter driving wheels, '54XX' Class pannier tanks with 5ft 2in diameter driving wheels and '64XX' Class pannier tanks with 4ft 7½in wheels were introduced for auto-train working. The '517s' and Metro tanks were becoming due for replacement and the famous Collett '48XX', later '14XX', series 0-4-2 was introduced as a direct replacement. The only other Great Western locomotives fitted for auto-working were some '45XX' and '55XX' Prairie tanks for use on re-organised services in South Wales in 1953. It is worth pointing out that the constituent South Wales railways had also made use of auto-trains, notably the Taff Vale and Rhymney Railways.

So much for the auto-fitted locomotives. Their accompanying auto-coaches came from a variety of sources and, like the railmotors, were designated as either 'branch' or 'suburban' types. Trailer No 1 was, for example, a unique matchboard-sided vehicle built in a similar style to railmotor No 1, for which it was originally constructed. Others were converted from clerestory coaching stock, the most notable of which were the Clifton Down sets, which were converted from suburban coaches.

However, by far the greatest proportion of these early auto-coaches came from the rebuilding of railmotors, a gradual process that began in the early years of the First World War and continued well into the 1930s. How vehicles were selected for rebuilding seems to lack logic as some of the earliest railmotors were still in service in the mid 1930s. Many of these conversions remained in service until the 1950s and some subsequently passed into departmental use.

The conversion of the railmotors meant that there was little need for new, specially designed auto-coaches to be built. However, three specific batches were built between the wars. These vehicles are very popular with modellers and, with a Collett '14XX', often form the clichéd Great Western branch line train on model railway layouts. They are often identified by their diagram numbers, both in detailed descriptions and in advertisements, particularly by model kit manufacturers. In order, therefore, to assist modellers to easily differentiate between the three new batches, the following brief descriptions refer to their Diagram numbers (see Table 4).

The first were 59ft 6in bow-ended saloons to diagram A.27; intended for branch line use, they lasted until 1960. The second batch of vehicles to diagram A.28 were longer, 62ft 8in, but had a similar usage and longevity as the diagram A.27 vehicles, spending most of their life in South Wales. The final batch of newly built pre-Second World War auto-coaches, to diagram A.30, were again 62ft 8in long, but with flush windows. They lasted until 1961.

Table 4: Auto-coaches

| Diagram No | Date built | Running Nos | Dimensions (ft in) | Comments |
|---|---|---|---|---|
| A | 1904 | 1 | 59 6 x 8 6 | |
| B | | 2 | 7 0¾ x 8 6¼ | |
| B | 1905 | 3-6 | 70 0 x 9 0 | |
| C | 1905 | 7-8 | 59 6 x 9 0 | For Lambourn Valley |
| D | 1905 | 9-10 | 70 0 x 9 0 | |
| E/F | 1905 | 11-13 | 70 0 x 9 0 | |
| G/G1/H | | 14-17 | 52¼ x 8 6¼ | Conversions from 52-foot 'Cornishman' 3rds |
| J/J1 | 1906 | 19-24 | 59 6 x 9 0 | |
| K/K1 | 1905 | 25-28 | 70 0 x 9 0 | |
| L | 1906 | 29-34 | 70 0 x 9 0 | |
| M/M1 | | 18-35 | 54¼ x 8 6¼ | Conversions from 54-foot clerestory 3rds |
| N | 1907 | 36-41 | 59 6 x 9 0 | |
| L | 1906 | 42-47 | 70 0 x 9 0 | |
| O | 1907 | 48 | 70 0 x 9 0 | One-off experimental (see text) |
| P | 1907 | 49-52 | 70 0 x 9 0 | |
| L | 1908 | 53-58 | 70 0 x 9 0 | |
| L | 1908 | 59-70 | 70 0 x 9 0 | |
| Q | 1909 | 71-72 | 70 0 x 9 0 | |
| R | 1909 | 73-74 | 70 0 x 9 0 | |
| T | 1911 | 75-80 | 70 0 x 9 0 | |
| U | 1912 | 81-92 | 70 0 x 9 0 | |
| Q | 1913 | 93-95 | 70 0 x 9 0 | |
| R | 1913 | 96-98 | 70 0 x 9 0 | |
| A.27 | 1929 | 159-170 | 59 6 x 9 0 | |
| A.28 | 1930 | 171-180 | 62 8 x 9 0 | |
| A.26 | 1930 | 181-185 | 70 0 x 9 0 | Ex-railmotors |
| A.29 | | 186 | | Ex-railmotor |
| A.30 | 1933 | 187-196 | 62 8 x 9 0 | |
| A.23 | 1934 | 197-198 | 70 0 x 9 0 | Ex-railmotors |
| A.26 | | 199, 200, 206 | 70 0 x 9 0 | Ex-railmotors |
| A.29 | | 201 | 70 0 x 9 0 | Ex-railmotor |
| A.31 | | 202-205 | 59 6 x 9 0 | Ex-railmotors |
| A.26 | 1936 | 210, 212-215 | 70 0 x 9 0 | Ex-railmotors |
| A.31 | | 211 | 59 6 x 9 0 | Ex-railmotor |
| A.29 | 1936 | 216-218 | 70 0 x 9 0 | Ex-railmotors |
| A.31 | | 219 | 59 6 x 9 0 | Ex-railmotor |
| E.147 | 1936 | 6818-6820 | 57 0 x 9 0 | |
| A.34 | 1939 | 1668-1671 | 57 0 x 8 11 | |
| A.38 | 1951 | 222-234 | 64 0 x 8 11 | |
| A.39 | 1951 | 220 | 64 0 x 8 11 | |
| A.40 | 1951 | 221 | 64 0 x 8 11 | |
| A.43 | 1954 | 235-244 | 64 0 x 8 11 | |

*Above* In 1961 '14XX' 0-4-2T No 1466 with a single coach at Uffculme on the Hemyock branch – the classic Great Western branch line train, frequently reproduced on model railway layouts. *Ray Ruffell, Silver Link collection*

*Below* A pannier tank stands with its auto-coach at the terminus of the Lambourn branch. In the foreground is a gas tank wagon used to replenish the gas supply reservoirs of gas-lit coaches. *Lens of Sutton*

The underside and a close-up of the driving end of auto-coach No 187, built to Diagram A.30 of 1933. This is an Airfix (Dapol) kit enhanced by an OO Dart Castings detailing pack, shown prior to painting. *Tony Wright*

One further series of new vehicles to a Great Western design was constructed after the Second World War, entering service in 1951. These were the Hawksworth vehicles Nos 220 to 234, intended to continue the new look set by his corridor stock. As already mentioned, Nos 220 and 221 were named 'Wren' and 'Thrush' respectively, the names being painted in Pullman style in large letters below the waistline, and they worked in the London area. All were withdrawn by the end of 1964. A further batch of ten, Nos 235-244, were built in this style in 1954.

The same traffic arrangements in the Cardiff area that led to the '45XX' and '55XX' conversions in 1953, also resulted in a number of Great Western suburban 3rds being converted for auto-train use – not as driving trailers, but as intermediate coaches, thus releasing driving trailers previously used for this purpose. In 1958 some suburban Brake 3rds were converted for use as driving trailers.

# Diesel railcars

The Great Western Railway's first diesel railcar, No 1, appeared in 1933 and began successful trials on the Southall branch. It was supplied by AEC, had bodywork by Park Royal Coachworks, and was a well streamlined vehicle, even to the extent of having enclosed lamps and entry steps covered by a hinged panel. The railcar was 62 feet long, accommodated 69 passengers, and had a maximum speed of 60mph.

There was at this period much interest in the success in Germany of the 'Flying Hamburger' diesel railcar services that were responsible for improving journey times on a number of services. The GWR, anxious as always to learn from others' examples, felt that there was merit in such vehicles, particularly on suburban services, and three further railcars, more powerful than the first, were ordered for the Birmingham-Cardiff service in anticipation of reducing journey times by as much as half an hour. These railcars had two engines and a top speed of 80mph; they had seating for 44 and a small buffet area at one end.

Three additional railcars of this type, but without the buffet area to provide greater passenger accommodation, were ordered, then, later, a further ten, three of which, Nos 10, 11 and 12, had toilet accommodation provided for service on longer routes, but passenger accommodation was reduced by one to 63.

Railcar No 17 was a parcels car used in the London area, while No 18 was the first to appear with conventional buffing and drawgear and had lower-ratio gearing to enable a trailer to be hauled. It was used on the Lambourn branch and between Reading and Basingstoke. The railcars built to this date had various configurations of engine and gearbox, and anyone interested in these aspects and seeking further details is referred to the books listed in the Select Bibliography.

Twenty further railcars were ordered in 1938. Beginning with No 19, a new, more angular style was adopted, familiar to modellers as being

Drawings and dimensions of 'the Great Western Railway Company's new stream-lined Buffet Rail Car', from *The Great Western Railway Magazine* of May 1934. There are seats for 44 passengers, and the buffet area, with its serving counter, is at the right-hand end.

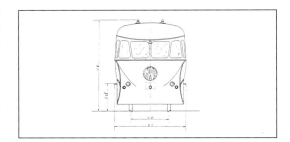

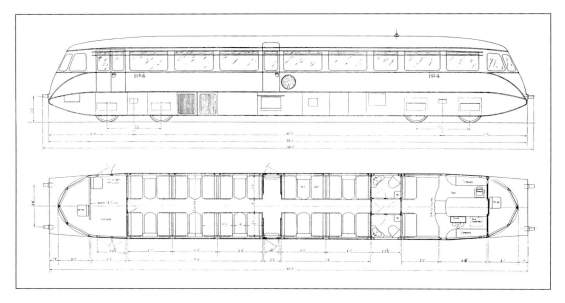

Eric Harrison's O gauge railcar No 19 on the Wolverhampton MRC's 'Woden Road' layout. The more angular styling of this 1938 batch of railcars is clearly seen. *Tony Wright*

the subject of excellent 2mm and 4mm scale models from Graham Farish and Lima respectively. These vehicles had Swindon-built bodies, but AEC continued to supply the transmissions and engines. Nos 19 and 20 had dual-ratio gearboxes enabling maximum speeds of either 40 or 60mph, depending on whether the vehicle was required to tow a trailer or not. No 34 was a parcels railcar, and again models of this are available, although as only one was built and its route limited, its use to modellers is debatable.

The last few vehicles, Nos 35 to 38, were single-ended with corridor connections between to enable them to run in multiple back-to-back or with a corridor coach in between.

**Table 5: Diesel railcars**

| Diagram No | Date built | Running Nos | Dimensions (ft in) |
|---|---|---|---|
| V | 1934 | 2-4 | 60 0 x 9 0 |
| W | 1935 | 5-7 | 60 0 x 9 0 |
| W | 1936 | 9, 13-16 | 60 0 x 9 0 |
| X | 1936 | 10-12 | 60 0 x 9 0 |
| Y | 1936 | 17 | |
| Z | 1937 | 18 | 60 0 x 9 0 |
| A.1 | 1941 | 19-33 | 62 0 x 9 0 |
| A.2 | 1941 | 34 | 62 0 x 9 0 |
| A.3 | 1942 | 36, 38 | 62 0 x 9 0 |
| A.4 | | 35, 37 | |

# 5
# LOCOMOTIVE AND COACH LIVERIES

Everybody knows that the Great Western ran green engines with chocolate and cream coaches, so why bother with a chapter on liveries? Well, within that broad outline lies a tremendous variety of detail, and indeed, in some cases, colour. Furthermore, wrong colours and incorrect livery details may well be conspicuous faults on otherwise excellent models, and it is a sad but true fact that a poor paint finish and incorrect or incomplete liveries mar a great many models. Hopefully, the details that follow will help overcome the latter problem and provide a quick and easy reference for the Great Western modeller. While perhaps Great Western liveries were somewhat more standard than most, the old adage still applies – for absolute accuracy, find a photograph of what you want to model at the time that your model is to represent. Black and white pictures may be more helpful here than you may at first imagine. The excellent HMRS publication *Great Western Way* is recommended as further reading and is a book no Great Western modeller should be without!

The dates given below for both locomotive and coach livery details are usually the dates at which changes were introduced. However, older livery styles often remained for many years after a new style was introduced because new styles were applied to new building and repaints as stock went into the works for major overhaul. Equally, styles that were not in vogue for more than a few years would, unless there was major building at the time, not have been very common, yet may have lasted for many years on the items so painted.

## Locomotive liveries

### Colours
The details of the earliest GWR locomotive liveries are somewhat uncertain, the earliest known official livery style dating from 1886. However, the details below for the period before this are believed to be accurate and, while this is not a popular modelling period, are included for completeness.

**1846-1866, Swindon:** *Smokebox and inside frames* Black; outside frames (loco and tender), dark brown lined yellow. *Boiler and firebox* a) wooden lagged, polished wood with brass boiler bands, b) plate covered, holly green with boiler bands lined in white at either edge. *Tender body* Holly green, panel lining in yellow. *Buffer beams* Red. *Wheels* Holly green, black tyres. *Coupling rods* Bosses polished, rest painted to match frames. Copper–capped chimneys appeared around 1855.

**Pre-1880, Wolverhampton:** *Smokebox* Black. *Boiler/body panels* Dark blue/green, boiler bands, borders and panels black edged in vermilion. *Outside frames* Dark brown, lined black and red. *Inside frames* Black.

**1880-1894, Wolverhampton:** *Body colour* Dark blue/green, black boiler bands, borders and panelling picked out in white. *Outside frames* Brown, edged black, picked out in vermilion; bosses (when not hidden) had black and red lines round edge, red innermost.

**1866-1881, Swindon:** *Main body and tender* Holly green bordered top and right-hand side with white line, bottom and left-hand side with black line edged with vermilion. *Panelling* Pea green bands. *Boiler* Holly green, bands black with white edges. *Wheels* Holly green with either black or bright polished tyres. *Buffer beams* Vermilion with black borders picked out in white. *Inside frames* Black outside, vermilion inside. *Outside frames* Umber with black border and vermilion line to inside.

Cast brass number plates were introduced around 1876, originally in two types of lettering; one continued in use, becoming standard to the end of Great Western steam.

Side tanks were painted with three panels originally, but later this was reduced to one large panel on Swindon locomotives. The numbers were in the centre. At Wolverhampton, however, the practice was to paint two panels with the numbers in the centre of the rearmost panel.

Tenders appeared with a variety of shapes and numbers of painted panels until about 1890, when the well-known three-panel scheme with the monogram in the centre panel was adopted.

**1881-1894, Swindon:** *Main body* Lighter green, boiler bands and borders black, picked out in chrome orange. *Buffer beams* Vermilion. *Wheels* Green with black tyres, then Indian red from 1886. *Inside frames* Black outside, vermilion inside. *Wheel splashers* Indian red, edged black with orange line between.

**1894-1914:** *1894* Middle chrome green adopted as standard green. Wolverhampton livery ceased to be used for repaints but it is likely that it could still be seen on locos for several years. *1900* Engine number appeared on front buffer beam. *1903* Wheel splashers green, with green line introduced on boiler bands between black and orange, giving characteristic orange/green/black/green/orange for boiler bands. *1905* Some auto-tanks brown (coach chocolate) lined out in orange, wheels and underframes black. *1906* Number plates removed from tanks to bunkers. Smaller tank locos had plates moved to rear of tanks. Underframes and wheels now painted black, orange lining retained. Familiar shade of green adopted. *1908* Practice of fixing works plates stopped, and works plates removed from locomotives that carried them.

**1914-1923:** *First World War* Economies forced the end of elaborate liveries and polished metal fittings. Some special liveries were introduced.

Dave Murdoch's O gauge '42XX' Prairie tank No 4206, built from a Gladiator kit, is in the pre-First World War lined green livery with the garter crest between the words 'Great Western', and the number plate on the bunker. The number also appears on the buffer beam. *Tony Wright*

*1915* Khaki-green body colour, black underframes and wheels, orange buffer beams, no lining. Some locos painted in this way retained copper-capped chimneys and polished brass safety valve covers. *1917* Reversion from khaki to green but seemingly a dull colour, not pre-war shade, otherwise as 1915 except all polished metal such as domes, etc, painted. *1918-1923* Plain unlined green livery retained. *1923* Lining out in pre-war style returned to express but not tank locos.

**1923-1942:** The livery for the period 1923-42 may be conveniently summarised as follows: **Express locomotives** *Middle chrome green* Basic body colour including splasher sides and cab fronts. *Black* Smokebox, underframes and wheels, cab roof, footplate tops and splasher top. *Vermilion* Buffer beams with single orange line to edge and round outer edge of buffer shanks. *Lining* Orange/green/black/green/orange (total width only 2¼in) around cab sides and for boiler bands; single orange line inside splasher side below beading and along edge of running plate; double orange lines to form panel on cylinders with single line to front and rear edges; no lining on firebox tops. Chimneys had copper caps and safety valve covers were polished brass. Familiar polished brass numerals on standard plate with black background and single orange line inside.

**Express locomotive tenders** *Middle chrome green* Body above running plate including flared coal rails. *Black* Outer beading, coal rail, tender top, running plate edge, tender frames and steps. *Vermilion* Buffer beams with single orange line inside. *Lining* Main body, coal rails and tender back had lining of orange/green/black/green/orange in panels round each area, as for locomotives; steps and running plate edged with single orange line.

**Mixed traffic and tank locomotives:** As express locos except no lining and, officially, no polished copper cap or chimney or brass safety valves. However, unofficially many of these lesser locos retained these features. No crest between words 'Great Western'; in 1934, words replaced with 'shirt button' monogram. Only Great Western locos painted black were some ROD 2-8-0s briefly in the 1930s, but they retained standard wording on tender side.

In 1928 the shade of green was changed and became slightly more yellow for newly introduced 'Castles' and other express types, eg 'Stars', 'Saints' and 'Counties'. Polished metalwork was also re-instated, except for the splasher beading.

**1942-1945:** *Second World War from 1942* As in First World War, economies forced changes in

A South Eastern Finecast OO 'King' built by Tony Wright and painted by Ian Rathbone, displaying a mid-1930s livery complete with 'shirt button' GWR roundel on the tender. *Tony Wright*

Bachmann's current ready-to-run 'Modified Hall' is finished in the post-war livery with 'G crest W' on the tender. *Tony Wright*

liveries, but not until after 1942. Between then and 1945 all repainted locomotives except 'Castles' and 'Kings' were in unlined green. *1945* Introduction of Hawksworth 'Counties' brought back lining (but not below footplate level) to principal express locos only.

**1945-1948:** *Express locomotives and tenders* As pre-war except no lining on black areas or buffer beams, but buffer beam numbers re-instated. Wartime restricted lettering on tender to initials only, 'G crest W', rather than full lettering. *Mixed traffic and tank locomotives* As pre-war, unlined green, lettered GWR; chimneys and safety valve casings again officially painted but some polished; buffer beam numbers applied again.

## Crests and lettering

The GWR coat of arms combined the arms of London and Bristol, and was first used encircled by a garter in the fashion of railway crests until around 1930.

In 1904 some tenders had the letters 'GWR', and a few had the garter crest, applied in place of the elaborate monogram that had been used earlier, when the garter crest had been placed on the splasher sides where their design allowed. However, by the end of 1904 the familiar 'Great garter crest Western' style became standard on tenders.

In 1906 tank locomotives bore the words

'Great Western' in similar style but without the garter crest, and later, but to a limited extent, the full 'Great crest Western'.

In the late 1920s the garter was removed from the coat of arms and the words 'Great Western' only applied to all but the most important classes. Then, around the mid-1930s, the 'shirt button' roundel was introduced, but with the advent of the Second World War it did not become universal. However, it was sufficiently applied to be considered by modellers of this period.

The application of simplified liveries in the Second World War introduced the letters 'GW' on repaints in two styles, one similar to pre-war Great Western lettering, the other a simple block style. Express classes had the simplified crest between the letters. The post-war Great Western livery saw the letters 'GWR' applied to tender and tank sides. In the early days of nationalisation a few locomotives had the words 'British Railways' in Great Western-style lettering.

## Nameplates and number plates

There were various styles and methods of numbering and naming locomotives before the familiar cast plates became standard. Up to 1876 it was the practice to paint numbers on standard gauge locomotives. Cast brass number plates were then introduced in two styles, the familiar and later standard type and the other with a

Tender livery variations: the elaborate pre-1904 monogram on the tender of *City of Truro*; 'Great Western' flanking the garter-less coat of arms on No 5029 *Nunney Castle*; and the post-war 'G coat of arms W' on No 6998 *Burton Agnes Hall*. *All Will Adams*

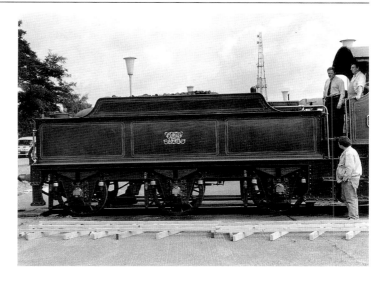

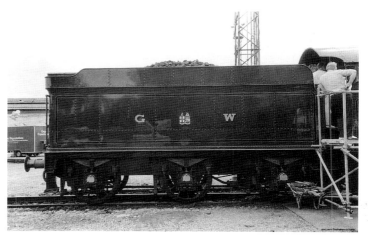

different style of lettering and numbering. Originally plates cast at Wolverhampton had 'Wolverhampton' beneath the numbers.

Curved number plates were used on the rear splashers of some 2-4-0s and brass figures without plates were tried on other locos.

There were three main types of nameplate: brass letters on either a curved or straight plate; nameplates curved to fit the splashers; and straight cast brass plates on either the boiler or tank side in the early days.

*Defiant*'s nameplate is curved to fit the centre splasher of the 'Castle'. This locomotive was named *Ogmore Castle* until 1941, when a dozen of the class were given wartime-relevant names, the 'Castle Class' suffix being added for clarity. *Will Adams*

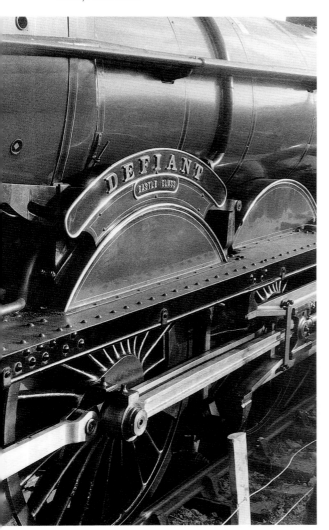

In 1893, raised brass letters on a curved steel strip fitted to the splasher side were introduced; the steel background was initially polished, but was later painted black. However, as wheel sizes reduced and splashers consequently became smaller, this style became impractical. A small number of plates, of varying types, were fitted outside the splasher until the familiar standard style was introduced in 1905.

### BR (Western Region) locomotive liveries

The very earliest indication of BR's ownership, before the crests evolved, and which appeared on few locomotives, were the words 'British Railways' in standard GWR lettering.

The adoption of standard liveries by British Railways followed a period of experimentation when various liveries were tried, including dark blue and light green on 'Kings' and 'Castles' respectively for a short period in 1948-49. The dark blue had LNWR-style red/cream/grey lining, as did the pale green, which was reminiscent of the Adams LSWR colour.

Brunswick green was ultimately adopted for express passenger classes, with GWR-style orange and black lining. Mixed traffic classes, which included the 'Counties', were black with LNWR red/cream/grey lining. However, by 1957, when some regional autonomy was being enjoyed in matters such as liveries, the mixed traffic locos and many others were coming out of the shops sporting lined green livery.

### BR diesel locomotive liveries

It is worth noting that in addition to the standard BR liveries, the 'Western' and 'Warship' diesel-hydraulics used by the Western Region also had other liveries. The 'Warships' appeared in green, maroon, and royal blue, while the 'Westerns' additionally appeared in a sand colour.

## Coach liveries

### Colours and lining

The famous 'chocolate and cream' livery dates back to 1864. However, it was actually originally chocolate and white, but the varnishes of the day gave it a cream tone, so this famous livery appeared almost by accident. Above the waist, including the roof, was white, and below the waist brown.

'47XX' 2-8-0 No 4702 in BR lined black livery. This 4mm model was built by Ted Kanas from a Martin Finney kit. *Tony Wright*

**1890-1898:** *Coach sides* Bottom and waist panels Windsor brown, panels above waist cream. *Droplights and bolection* Varnished mahogany or Venetian red. *Coach ends* Windsor brown, mouldings black. *Roof* White, brown between cantrail and rainstrip. *Clerestory side panelling* Lines as body upper panels. *Underframe* Windsor brown. *Bogies and running gear* Black. *Wheels:* Black (wooden panels of Mansell wheels varnished wood or Venetian red). *Lining* Body mouldings black, edges lined in gold, fine brown line on upper cream panels just in from moulding. *Lettering* Numbers in gold shaded black, 2in high in panels below cantrail, and usually appearing three times on each side, twice on brake coaches. *Class designation* Egyptian-style gold shaded black in waist panels on doors. Restaurant and sleeping cars had designation in waist panels also in this style. GWR monogram in lower panels, two on each side.

**1898-1907:** As the earlier livery except clerestory side panels were painted brown without lining. Underframe colour changed to black at some time during this period.

**1902 experimental livery:** Several vehicles were painted brown all over body. From 1905 a larger monogram, similar to that used on locomotives, was introduced, but was soon replaced with the garter crest placed centrally in lower panels.

**1907-1908:** Coach ends now black; numbers moved to waist board from cantrail.

**1908-1912:** Coaches painted chocolate lake but lettering, insignia, etc, remained unaltered. Lining now yellow ochre.

**1912:** Brown shade changed to crimson lake.

**1913:** New steel-panelled 'Toplights' had imitation panelling painted on sides.

**1914-1918:** No change during First World War except that clerestory lights were painted over.

**1923-1942:** Passenger coach liveries during this period can be summarised as follows (but see notes following): *Roof gutters* Chocolate. *Below gutters to waist level* Cream *Waist to bottom of coach side* Chocolate. *Underframe, bogies and wheels* Black (from 1927 oil boxes had tops painted bright blue for identification). *Window surrounds* Black. *Droplights* Indian red. *Lettering* Egyptian-style gold, shaded black; 'Great Western' up to 1928 separated by full garter crest, afterwards by new coat of arms; from 1934 'shirt button' monogram applied.

In the 1930s some suburban and local stock was painted all over chocolate.

Auto-trailers and PBVs used on main-line expresses were finished as the coaches, but from the early 1930s the majority of PBVs were painted all over brown, but continued the style of lettering. The ends of auto-trailers were painted as a continuation of the sides.

Steam railmotors sported the various coach liveries used during their lifetime but with large numbers in the waist panels.

**1922-1927:** Cream destination boards with black lettering also introduced. New 1925 bow-ended stock had painted imitation panelling, but this was short-lived.

**1927-1930:** Two-tone chocolate and cream without lining. In 1927 garter replaced with two-shield crest.

**1930-1933:** Simple lining scheme introduced to top and bottom of waist panels and at extreme ends, forming a long 'panel' down length of coach some 7½in wide. Lining gold/black. Word 'Third' dropped from doors.

**1934:** Buffet cars had cream panel in waist with words 'Buffet Car'. Other more usual lettering for special vehicles was in 3⅛in gold Egyptian letters, shaded black. 'Super Saloons' had names on centre of coach below waist.

**1936:** 'Third' re-introduced on doors of 'Sunshine' stock.

**1939-1945:** Roofs were dark grey. From 1942 repainted coaches appeared in red/brown with a single orange line along the waist.

**1945-1948 (see also note below):** *Coach body colours* Chocolate and cream as earlier, 7in chocolate band below roof, cream to waist, chocolate below waist. *Lining* Black and gold central panel and coach ends. *Underframes, bogies and coach ends* Black. *Roof* Black or dark grey. *Lettering* 'Great Western' in middle of body below waist, split by crest flanking coat of arms in most important stock.

**1946-1948:** Various experimental liveries tried, but two-tone livery restored with new Gill Sans typeface. Words 'Great Western' with arms of London and Bristol between in centre lower panels of coaches. Roofs remained dark grey. *Lining* Horizontal brown band 7in wide at top edge of coach side edged at meeting with lower cream panels with gold/black lines. Two horizontal lines of black inside a fine gold line

The current Bachmann Collett coach in the post-1934 livery with 'shirt button' monogram. *Tony Wright*

7in apart at top of brown lower panels. *Wheels, bogies and underframes* Black.

**Auto-coaches:** Chocolate and cream including ends, as coaches.

**PBVs:** Chocolate and cream full livery, but monogram replaced by coat of arms on nose ends and 'Great Western' separated by crest on sides.

## BR (Western Region) coach liveries

Some Great Western coaches inevitably received early experimental liveries such as 'plum and spilt milk'. However, carmine and cream was adopted as standard. Some vehicles appeared with the last GWR-style 'double lines' along the waist and 'W'-prefixed numbers to the left-hand side.

Lining was gold/black along the cantrail and gold/black/gold along the waist line between the colours.

**1949:** Crimson adopted for new corridor vehicles, lined with horizontal black and yellow line at cantrail and gold/black/gold along waistline. Auto-trailers were painted standard crimson and cream livery, though some appeared in non-corridor lined crimson or even unlined crimson.

**1956:** BR Mk 1 stock, ex-GWR Restaurant Cars, 'Super Saloons' for principal expresses and Inspection Saloons painted a version of chocolate and cream but not the same colours as pre-war Great Western.

**1962:** Autonomy led to discontinuation of all repaints in BR standard crimson lined in gold and black along waist and cantrail.

Diesel railcars, which in Great Western days had sported the simplified chocolate and cream livery of the 1930s, with large numbers, appeared after the war in the lined carmine and cream livery and later diesel-unit green, with standard DMU lining and front-end 'whiskers'.

## Coach interiors

It is quite likely that in 4mm and 7mm scales some representation of coach interiors will be required. It will be sufficient for most purposes to identify the main colours/finishes used in the decoration of coaches, and these are simplistically summarised as follows:

**Interior woodwork/panelling:** *1890-1936* Walnut, mahogany or dark oak (for modelling purposes a dark red/brown will do). *1936-1946* Birchwood (pale green/yellow). *1946-1948* Maple (pale golden brown). *1948-1950* Cream enamelled panelling.

**Trim:** *1890-1939* Lighter woods such as sycamore or light oak (light green/brown). *1939-1948* Cream/blue. *1948-1950* Chocolate enamelled material.

**Seating:** Coach seating varied in colour and material over the years and between classes. For modelling purposes a general idea of colour is adequate.

The earliest colours were crimson in 1st Class, and brown in 2nd and 3rd Classes. Subsequently various colours were used, including brown, blue and green for 1st Class and various browns for other classes.

Around 1900 the upholstery was dark green in 1st Class, brown patterned in 2nd Class and dark red patterned in 3rd. From 1911 the colour for 3rd class was either blue/red or red/black patterned cloth.

Stock built between 1922 and 1929 was dark brown in 1st Class and red patterned in 3rd. Between 1929 and 1936 the colours were beige/black in 1st and grey/black in 3rd. In 1936 brighter colours were adopted, blue/green tartan in 1st Class and orange/brown patterned material in 3rd.

Post-war coaches had upholstery in dark blue with a fawn pattern in the 1st Class accommodation, a similar colour but a different pattern for 3rd class smoking accommodation, and fawn/red in smoking compartments.

# 6
# FREIGHT TRAFFIC, GOODS WAGONS AND 'BROWN' VEHICLES

This chapter outlines briefly the system of freight operation on the Great Western Railway and the development of traffic and vehicles. It is hoped that this sketch will better enable modellers to portray goods services on their layout and in particular to achieve proportionately the correct type of vehicles.

We begin with a few facts that may dispel some of the common myths held by railway modellers about freight traffic.

## Traffic development and organisation

First, 90 per cent of Great Western wagon stock before the Second World War was open merchandise stock or vans. In 1902 there were 54,161 merchandise wagons, 2,585 loco and coal wagons, 9 loco vans and 2,281 engineers' vehicles, a total of 59,036 vehicles, and this figure steadily increased.

The Grouping of 1923 increased the Great Western Railway's total stock, including absorbed wagons, to 96,501 despite the fact that the immediate post-First World War years had seen the widespread replacement of older 19th-century low-sided vehicles with larger, more modern open wagons and vans. Much of the absorbed stock was soon condemned, and by 1926 the wagon stock stood at 88,580.

The vast majority of wagons used prior to the Second World War for carrying minerals, particularly coal, coke and iron ore, were privately owned by mines or distributors and merchants. The figure in the 1930s is in the order of 5 to 1 private ownership to railway ownership of mineral wagons; in 1938 there were in mainland Britain 660,155 railway-owned wagons and 583,789 private owner wagons.

In 1938, ownership of wagons by the Great Western Railway was as follows:

| Wagon type | No in stock |
| --- | --- |
| Open wagons | 47,385 |
| Covered wagons | 27,787 |
| Cattle trucks | 3,070 |
| Rail and timber trucks | 2,367 |
| Special wagons | 2,318 |
| Brake-vans | 2,311 |
| Mineral wagons | 1,215 |
| | |
| Total | 86,453 |

These figures demonstrate clearly the few mineral wagons owned by the company.

Mineral wagons were very similar in appearance to open merchandise wagons. They carried coal and other minerals, but not loco coal, for which special wagons were used. Mineral wagons can usually be distinguished from open merchandise wagons by the drop-side doors, which do not continue to the top of the side. The inclusion of an end door is also a good indication of a mineral wagon.

Special wagons included vehicles such as creosote or gas oil wagons, etc. The comparatively high number of cattle trucks reflects the importance of this traffic on the Great Western Railway and the rural locations, particularly in the West Country, served by the railway. Milk traffic to London and other major cities was also important; various vans in the 'brown vehicle' category were built for the conveyance of milk churns. Later, four-wheel and six-wheel glass-lined tankers were introduced for this traffic.

Coal from the vast South Wales coalfield was undoubtedly the main single commodity freight traffic handled by the railway and, as has already been mentioned, the bulk of this was conveyed in 10-ton and 12-ton private owner wagons often made up into slow trains comprising in excess of 60 wagons.

Until the establishment of the common user principle during the First World War, railway-owned wagons operating on another company's system had to be returned to the owning company, loaded or not, within five days, or a daily fine was imposed by the Railway Clearing House (RCH).

The common user principle created a pool of unfitted open vehicles and closed merchandise wagons that became interchangeable throughout the mainland, so that any company's wagon could be loaded and dispatched from anywhere. The number of vehicles agreed for inclusion in this pool by the various companies was in proportion to the freight traffic handled. After the Grouping, the wagons pooled were as follows:

| | |
|---|---|
| Great Western | 65,000 |
| LMS | 217,000 |
| LNER | 170,000 |
| Southern | 29,000 |

Wagons not used in the pool were marked 'Return to GWR – Not Common User', and this marking was carried after 1923 on all specially constructed or used freight stock.

### Traffic organisation

The first vacuum-fitted express goods trains were operated by the Great Western Railway in the 1890s, but the major developments in this type of train, to link up major parts of the system and convey general merchandise for next-day delivery, occurred in the late 1920s. This was quickly followed by the development of the express vacuum-fitted freight train in the 1930s and all its attendant publicity in an attempt to stem the advancing tide of road competition – freight tonnage handled by the railway was steadily declining during the 1930s, losing out to road traffic.

The Publicity Department excelled itself in promoting these fast vacuum-fitted freight services, adopting unofficial nicknames for the various trains, making great play of the GWR's services, and producing a booklet especially for potential customers. Samples of the 75 names are given in Appendix 2.

From the 1920s vacuum-fitted express goods trains were operated by the GWR to link up major parts of the system and convey general merchandise for next-day delivery. This painted advertising sign was photographed at Stroud as recently as 1970. *Will Adams*

Specific loads based on numbers of 10-ton wagons and their equivalents, together with route conditions, etc, were linked to locomotive tractive effort, and the Great Western produced a ready-reckoner of motive power loads for freight services. The company also identified specific types of train, ranging from the fast vacuum-fitted, which averaged 50 wagons behind a '47XX' or 'Castle' at average speeds in excess of 40mph, down to long mineral trains comprising in excess of 70 unfitted wagons struggling along at no more than 25mph. Between these two examples there were various permutations and classifications. Where vacuum-fitted stock was included on fast services, the vacuum-fitted vehicles were marshalled next to the engine.

The greatest advantages in speed, economy and ease of handling occurred in moving full or nearly full wagon loads between major centres. However, freight patterns did not all conveniently fall in with this orderly plan, and the most difficult and uneconomical scenario was the movement of smaller loads. The Great Western, having taken care of the express services between centres, evolved a system whereby small loads were forwarded to one of a number of tranship centres, the idea being to re-concentrate and despatch full or almost full wagon loads. Additionally there were many cross-country services used for gathering small loads that otherwise would have been retained at central points until wagon loads had accumulated for a given destination. Similarly, there were the well-known pick-up freights, setting down and collecting freight at wayside stations.

Successful operation of the freight side of railway traffic relied on the co-ordination and distribution of wagon stock to meet traffic demands with the minimum empty wagon time or movement. However, as goods services did not always fall into convenient patterns, empty wagon movements were necessary to balance out workings. Industrial regions sent out far more goods than they received, whereas, except at peak crop times for produce such as broccoli in Cornwall, rural areas received more than was sent. A general pattern was that loaded wagons moved in greater numbers north-south than south-north, and consequently the Great Western Railway dealt with a great many LMS and LNER wagons.

In 1945 the Great Western further changed its goods distribution and handling system in an attempt to streamline and speed freight traffic. The whole system was zoned, each zone having a railhead and sub-stations; loading was therefore concentrated at fewer centres. Goods dropped off by local services were transferred by road to the sub-stations where full wagon loads were made up. Where the goods were not sufficient for a full wagon load they were conveyed by road to the main railhead in that zone. Goods were collected there from various despatch points, for wagon loads could be more readily assembled from cumulative receipts. Where direct transit by rail was not possible, the Great Western's motor lorry service filled in the gaps, and it was even likely that small quantities of goods travelling within a zone might be carried entirely by road. This scheme, zonal collection and delivery, was later to be taken up by British Railways.

# Goods stock

Changes to the system and methods of operation were also reflected in the development of specific goods stock and services, notably container traffic, which was developed to suit a wide variety of loads from general merchandise to ventilated and insulated containers for perishable goods and meat. Special containers were developed for bicycles and for bulk liquid chemicals. Modellers should note that all container wagons, known as Conflats, except a batch built during the Second World War, the Conflat As, were vacuum-fitted and had lamp irons.

The GWR also experimented with 20-ton steel coal wagons and tried hard to get these adopted as standard, but the attempt was unsuccessful, the wooden 10-ton variety remaining the most common private owner wagon.

The majority of early wagons were open, low-sided affairs usually 15ft 6in long with sides two or three planks high; later 16-foot-long four-plank wagons became the norm for general merchandise.

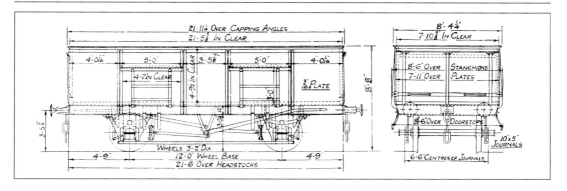

The GWR hoped that its new 20-ton steel coal wagon would become the standard, but the wooden 10-ton variety remained the most common private owner wagon. *Great Western Railway Magazine, 1925/Philip J. Kelley collection*

Attempts were made by the Railway Clearing House to achieve standardisation among wagons, not least in the use of standard components that would enable repairs and maintenance to be easily undertaken throughout the country, no matter what system the wagon was on, and the Great Western Railway was one of the companies that adopted the 17ft 6in RCH underframe. The wheelbase of open merchandise wagons and vans was 9 feet until 1933, after which the 10-foot wheelbase became standard. Modellers should note that the majority of ordinary vehicles, and particularly general merchandise open wagons and private owner wagons, even in the early British Railways period, were of 9-foot wheelbase, whereas the majority of ready-to-run models are of 10-foot wheelbase underframe wagons, usually the later standard RCH type.

The building and replacement of wagons was a continuous process, but not all wagons replaced in general service were scrapped. Many old vehicles found their life lengthened sometimes after refurbishment, finding use in internal duties such as carrying sand for brake-van sanding gear or within the various dock complexes. Vehicles used in this way were usually marked with some restriction such as 'For use at X only'.

The use of steel-bodied wagons was not confined to the 20-ton coal wagons mentioned earlier. The Great Western Railway designed various types of iron-bodied vehicles, perhaps the best known of which were the 'Iron Minks', first built in the 1880s. Open wagons for coal and ballast followed in the 1890s, but after the Minks F of 1911 wood became the standard material for van bodies, although various hopper and loco coal wagons were built with steel bodies, including the aforementioned 20-ton coal wagons.

Iron may seem an unusual choice for goods wagons, but surprisingly all iron vehicles had a lower tare weight (ie net unladen weight) than equivalent wooden-bodied wagons. The initial building cost was higher, but maintenance costs lower.

Tank wagons are popular with modellers, but most were privately owned; railway-owned tankers

*Right* Two GWR Conflats from the 1930s, vacuum-fitted wagons designed to carry containers adapted for various loads, in this case an FX insulated container for perishable goods and a K-type container for furniture removals. Note that both carry 'Not Common User' plates, so could not be used by another railway company to carry a return load. Also note the open five-plank general merchandise wagons in the right background of each photograph. *Both Philip J. Kelley collection*

carried such materials as creosote, locomotive department water, gas, etc. The telegraphic code for these was Cordon. The last development was demountable tanks on flat wagons, which could also be used on road transport and were designed for door-to-door conveyance of bulk liquids, particularly chemicals.

The modeller not familiar with Great Western wagons may well be faced with references to vehicles such as MOGO, Conflat, ASMO, etc. These were telegraphic codes used by the Great Western to identify wagons. The code was sub-divided between different vehicles used for the same purpose, for example Conflats were flat wagons for use with containers, whereas Conflat As were similar vehicles without vacuum braking or lamp brackets. Goods wagons are often identified by their telegraphic code and accordingly, to assist modellers, Appendix 3 lists the codes used.

A wooden-bodied van and an 'Iron Mink' in EM gauge by Rob Kinsey. Redundant bodies of the latter type were often subsequently used for huts and sheds. *Tony Wright*

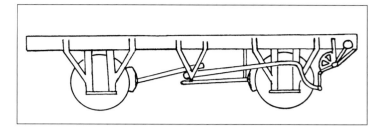

Figure 2: Sketch showing the outward appearance of the Dean-Churchward wagon brake. Note the handle and ratchet at the right-hand end – turning the handle released the brake, while it could be locked on with the ratchet rather than the lever arrangement, which required the lever to be locked in place with a pin.

Various types of brakes were used by the Great Western on its goods stock, and one variety, the Dean-Churchward pattern, is shown in Figure 2.

Everyone knows that Great Western brake-vans were called Toads, but what may not be so well known is that there were several varieties of Toad, some constructed for special purposes. To describe these vehicles fully would require a chapter in itself – let it suffice here to differentiate between the main varieties.

Vehicles 20 feet long on 13-foot wheelbases with 6ft 6in verandahs were built from 1880 to the First World War, after which 24-foot-long, 16-foot-wheelbase vehicles with 8ft 6in verandahs were built to nationalisation. Twenty-ton brake-vans became standard, the early 10-ton or 12-ton varieties not being much use for stopping longer, heavier trains. Indeed, 24-ton six-wheel vehicles were built in 1901 for heavy coal trains. Four special vans were built for the limited clearances on the Pontnenynnydd branch and were replaced by four new vehicles built in 1949.

Permanent way brake-vans and ballast brake-vans with spreaders were also built, as were special brake-vans with closed-in verandahs for use in the Severn Tunnel to protect guards from the worst effects of smoke and fumes.

## Goods wagon liveries

Dark grey was adopted as the basic wagon livery in 1898, prior to which goods stock had been red with black ironwork. It is worth noting, however, that while the grey colour was standard, goods stock was not subject to regular cleaning, nor did it receive repaints as often as locomotives and coaches. Furthermore, wagons were often patched up and painted away from Swindon as a result of repairs. They also suffered not only from the weather but from the dust and stains of the goods they carried, as well as wear

and tear from continual loading, unloading, shunting and generally being roughly treated. A train or goods siding on a model railway containing wagons that are clean and of a uniform shade and weathering – including private owner vehicles – is clearly not representative of the real Great Western or its successor!

The basic dark grey body colour was also applied to the underframe. However, certain other vehicles were painted in different colours. Meat vans, MICAs and water tank wagons were painted white to keep them cool, while engineers' and permanent way wagons and creosote tanks were painted black. Van roofs were white.

As regards lettering, company ownership in broad gauge days was identified with 5in white sans serif lettering complete with full stops applied to the lower left-hand side of the body, with the running number at the opposite end in similar style. Load, tare and special markings such as 'Return to X Great Western Railway' were applied in italics, to which any wagon names or departmental ownership were added in block capitals. Where vehicles needed special operating instructions, these appeared on a cast plate fixed to the wagon. This plate was black with white lettering.

From about 1898, on new wagons, the initials 'GWR', load and tare were on cast plates fixed to the lower plank of wooden-bodied vehicles and to the solebars on others. Special instructions were painted in italics as earlier.

From 1904, 25in-high initials 'GW' were introduced, the wagon running number appearing in the left-hand corner and on the ends, in a central position, or on the buffer beam on flat or well-type wagons. The right-hand corner carried, in italic script, the load and tare; where there was no room for the standard

*Above*  8-ton cattle wagon No 106324 at Swindon, in the standard grey livery. Note the large 'GW' initials, the wagon running number at the left-hand end and in the centre of the ends, and, in italic script, the load and tare at the right-hand end. *Philip J. Kelley collection*

*Below*  8-ton fruit van No 106193, showing a paint date of 1939. From 1936 the lettering was reduced to 5 inches high and was moved to the left-hand side above the load and running number. *Philip J. Kelley collection*

lettering, reduced lettering was applied. Telegraph codes also appeared on wagons at this time.

The Grouping coincided with a reduction in the size of lettering to 16in, and from 1936 this was further reduced to 5in and moved to the left-hand side above the load and running number. Lettering was white, except on the white-bodied MICAs where it was red, and on water tankers, which had black letters.

During the First World War, the 'Not Common User' wording was replaced on repainted wagons with four white Xs. During and after the Second World War, patch painting and bare planks after repairs were the order of the day. Lettering, in the lower left-hand side of the wagon, was small at 5in.

Wagon tarpaulins were of a very dark grey to black appearance and bore white lettering with code numbers and the large initials 'GW' in the standard style. Later, with the introduction of the 'shirt button' monogram, a white version of this replaced the initials on new sheets.

Even discounting 'any old vehicle lettered GW', the modeller is well served by good ready-to-run GWR vehicles and inexpensive quality kits. The more specialist etched brass and cast kits open up a world that covers, at least in 4mm and increasingly 7mm scale, a vast collection of vehicles. Furthermore, there is ample opportunity to convert and detail ready-to-run GWR models into other types, and the model railway press continues to describe conversions ranging from the simple repaint and lettering of the Dapol BR cattle wagon kit to more complex and quite comprehensive rebuilds.

## 'Brown' vehicles

In addition to what might be called ordinary goods stock, there were a variety of wagons that often travelled in passenger trains, and these were painted brown. They ranged from open carriage trucks and horse-boxes through to the well-known Siphons and Monsters.

The date from which these vehicles were singled out for the brown livery is unclear; 1916 or thereabouts is often quoted, but there are indications that the practice originated much earlier. The vans and carriage trucks were numbered in a separate series from ordinary goods stock and are often considered with coaches.

The early Siphons were slatted for the conveyance of milk in churns, the slatted sides being an attempt to keep the churns cool before the advent of insulated and later refrigerated vehicles. The first Siphons were four-wheel vehicles built in the 1870s, and these were followed by further examples and later six-wheel Siphon Cs, which lasted into BR days. The Siphon G is represented by excellent 4mm scale models, and originated in 1913, as did the much larger-looking Monster with its high roof; Siphon Hs also had this high roof.

It is interesting to note that some Python As (covered carriage trucks) were specially strengthened to carry elephants in 1914, an example of the versatility of many 'brown' vehicles and the variety of the loads they were required to carry. The conveyance of horses in horse-boxes, vehicles on open carriage trucks and CCTs, and milk in various types of Siphon are typical goods uses of passenger train services.

Many passenger brake vans not used on prestige main-line expresses were also painted brown, but retained passenger-coach-style lettering and numbering. Later, true 'brown' vehicles were gangwayed vehicles, such as the longer-bodied Siphon Gs, of which there were both outside-framed and smooth-sided varieties, and for both of which excellent ready-to-run models are available in 4mm scale. The latter type had electric lights and was often used for parcel traffic in express trains.

Some 'brown' vehicles were used for specific traffic services such as sausage and bacon conveyance, and carried special boards on their sides indicating their usage.

These 'brown' vehicles are very attractive and popular with modellers. For those fortunate enough to have a main-line layout, a train of the various Siphons, perhaps mixed with other passenger and luggage vans on a parcels or perishable train, makes an intriguing sight.

A point to watch on some of the ready-to-run vehicles is the fitting of incorrect bogies. However, these can easily be changed for the correct type. The Hornby Siphon G is an example; the substitution of correct American-

A 'Bloater A' fish van photographed at Swindon in 1919. *Philip J. Kelley collection*

type bogies can transform the appearance of this otherwise superb model.

### 'Brown' vehicle liveries

These vehicles had chocolate brown bodywork, including the ends, with white or grey roofs. The lettering style and principles were the same as for ordinary goods stock and the telegraph code and numbering were carried in yellow ochre, and in the corresponding place on the body. The letters 'GW' were superseded after 1934 by the 'shirt button' GWR monogram, placed centrally.

## Modelling goods traffic

It is hoped that the early part of this chapter, discussing the traffic and operation of freight services on the Great Western Railway, will have helped to set the scene for the authentic operation of freight on a model railway. Here are a few guidelines for modelling GWR goods traffic.

- However attractive the specialist vehicles available to the modeller might be, they represent a very, very small proportion of the total wagon stock, and unless you are operating a through main or secondary line, or you have a specialist industry or facilities requiring these vehicles, such as a dairy or steelworks, or you operate an urban terminus that may have, say, a milk or parcels depot, these vehicles, including milk tanks, should generally be avoided.

- If you want to convey milk traffic on your branch line and have not modelled a dairy or creamery, use small Siphons, such as Siphon Cs (which would convey milk in churns) rather than milk tanks.

- The majority of general merchandise conveyed before the last war was conveyed in open wagons, which may or may not have been sheeted over, depending on the load.

Basic goods wagons are all that is needed to create authentic freight operations. A cattle wagon like that seen in the photograph on page 73 is one of four in a typical cut being propelled by a small Prairie on Philip George's EM 'Coedway' layout. Note the 'foreign' LNER wagon. *Tony Wright*

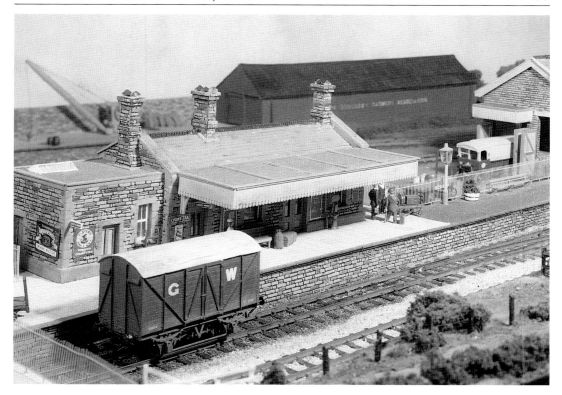

Unless your layout features a through main or secondary line, or you have a specific industry or facilities requiring specialised vehicles, such as a dairy or steelworks, stick to general merchandise wagons, both opened and covered, which handled the majority of everyday traffic. Note the GWR delivery lorry at the goods shed on the right of this photograph of Mike Corps's TT 'West Harptree' layout. *Tony Wright, courtesy British Railway Modelling*

- Private owner and GWR wagons are not enough to represent a true picture. Other companies' general merchandise wagons should be represented by a vehicle or two from, particularly, the LMS, which had large borders with the GWR, and perhaps, if the layout is set in the West Country, the Southern.

- The various Siphons, although ostensibly for milk traffic, were also used for the conveyance of many other commodities.

- Avoid special brake-vans, attractive as they may be – unless you are modelling the Severn Tunnel!

- Cattle was a very important commodity; whole trains of several wagons could run to the smallest rural branch line station on a market day and often snarled up regular workings. There are several types of GWR cattle wagons available in kits or from easy conversions, and these would be the general rule: 'foreign' vehicles would be very much in the minority in most areas, although more common in others.

# 7
# BUILDINGS AND STRUCTURES

It has been said that the true test of the authenticity of a model railway is to remove from it all the locomotives and items of rolling-stock, then view it. If the company, location and, to a lesser extent, period of the model is clearly evident, then the model has indeed succeeded. Thus, stations and other structures are very important aspects in creating authenticity on a model railway. Those on the Great Western were as diverse as the many lines it operated, despite various 'standard' designs that emerged from time to time.

In this chapter there is a brief outline of styles and major developments in Great Western architecture in so far as they relate to the types of facilities in which the space-starved modeller is likely to be interested. The reader will also find a few scale drawings and sketches of architectural features; these are provided not to enable a finely detailed model of a particular building to be made, but to provide a source to enable modellers to adapt and prepare their own designs to suit their needs. There are also photographs of various structures, both prototype and model. For those wishing to model specific locations and buildings, excellent histories and detailed drawings have been published on many areas of the Great Western Railway, and some are listed in the Select Bibliography; there are also regular articles to be found in the model railway press, where there has been an abundance of drawings of GWR structures over the years. Your local library should be able to obtain for you the now out-of-print and sorely missed Leleux Index of Model Railway Drawings, which will save much hard work and avoid the 'hit and miss' search if you have particular structures in mind. Ian Allan produced a similar book, which only covers more recent years but is nevertheless a useful source.

This chapter will not deal with signal boxes or signalling, as these will be covered in Chapter 8.

## Passenger stations

Brunel, in the early years of the Great Western Railway, laid down certain basic styles for his stations, which were adapted to suit particular locations. Basically there were two designs of Brunel station. One was the 'roadside' station, initially appearing on the Thames Valley line, of red brick with stone plinths, quoins and window surrounds, and steeply pitched roofs, topped with ornate chimneys and awnings on all sides. These 'roadside' stations were loosely 'Elizabethan' in style and, as the railway spread, the basic design was adapted to suit local conditions and, above all, local materials; for example, in Gloucestershire many were built in local stone. The second design was much removed from the first, following classical Italianate lines. These buildings became known as the 'chalet' style. This type of building was quite widespread and appeared in brick and, less commonly, timber.

Another Brunellian feature, the train shed, appears in matching style at Chard, and of more simple construction at many other locations. Perhaps the best known train shed of all was at Ashburton, a model of which is illustrated here and on pages 124-5. The purpose of the train shed was to give maximum protection from the elements to passengers, allowing them to move from waiting room to train under cover.

The Brunel Italianate design was perpetuated in a later, but uncommon, 'standard' style. These buildings had arched windows and elaborate wooden valances, and introduced cast columns to support the canopy.

The period that followed the Brunel era saw a

Station buildings on the Great Western were as diverse as the many lines it operated, and here are three that are distinctive yet somehow also typical. The first is the quaint building at the terminus of the Watlington branch, in brick with stone dressings; the structure at the end of the siding on the left is a carriage shed. The second photograph shows the rather more austere stone-built station building at Fairford at the terminus of the East Gloucestershire Railway, with its attendant cluster of corrugated buildings, including a 'Pagoda' hut, signal box and goods shed. *Both Lens of Sutton*

*Above* Another variation on the theme: a slightly larger and more elegant stone-built country station with canopy and Station Master's accommodation above modelled in O gauge by Allan Downes. *Tony Wright*

*Below* Model – or the real thing? Expert modelling and expert photography combine to produce an astonishingly lifelike view of Ashburton as modelled by Chris Lammacraft in EM. Note the train shed spanning the platform and tracks, as mentioned in the text. *Tony Wright, courtesy Model Rail*

general growth in the size of canopies and a change in their design, achieved through the use of steelwork. Many stations of this period had platform surfaces adjacent to the buildings in engineers blue brick.

The next design was introduced in the 1880s and followed on from the 'chalet' style. These buildings were ornately decorated, very much in line with what might be termed restrained Victorian style. They provided substantial accommodation for railway business, but not, alas, for the staff. The main features of these buildings were the small but heavily constructed porch over the entrance to the booking office on the approach side, the recessed front wall on the platform side and the substantial awning. The awning was supported on steel girders and there was decorative wooden valancing. Where the steelwork came through, the girder ends were capped with a lion mask gargoyle. There was a bay window at one end of the building, in the waiting room (see Figure 3).

A further 'standard' design of limited use was introduced in the late 19th century and was the

Figure 3: A development of the 'standard' design, showing the road-side porch and bay window features.

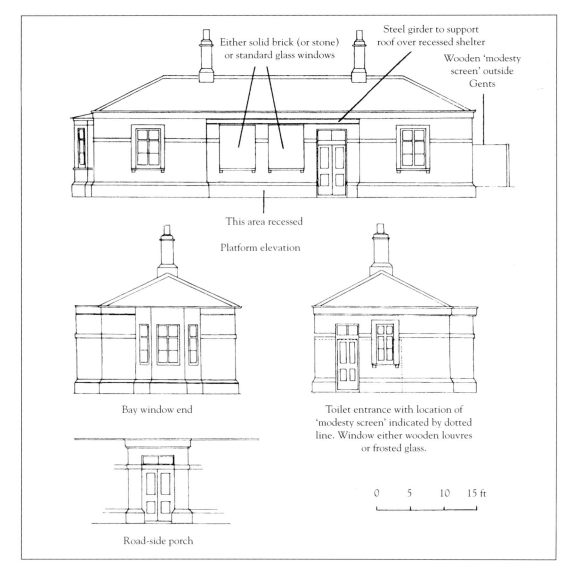

Either solid brick (or stone) or standard glass windows

Steel girder to support roof over recessed shelter

Wooden 'modesty screen' outside Gents

This area recessed

Platform elevation

Bay window end

Toilet entrance with location of 'modesty screen' indicated by dotted line. Window either wooden louvres or frosted glass.

0    5    10    15 ft

Road-side porch

first to move away from the influence of Brunel's Gothic or Italianate styles. These buildings were of distinctive cream sanitary glazed bricks with red brick decorations. There was also decorative stonework on sills, lintels and window and door surrounds. The buildings of this period had square, slate-covered turrets, tapering steadily inwards to the top. There was also much decorative ironwork on the roof.

The first of the 'standard' designs to see widespread use was introduced in the last years of the 19th century. Standardisation was an important consideration and the design of this building was such that it could be adapted, shortened or enlarged to suit a variety of locations and needs. It was of much simpler appearance, built round a combination of standard bays. Standard factory-manufactured doors and windows and joinery, facilitating modification and extension, were a feature introduced with this design, which appeared in a variety of configurations (see Figure 4).

Figure 4: An earlier type of 'standard' building, brick-built with stone dressing, hip roof and canopy.

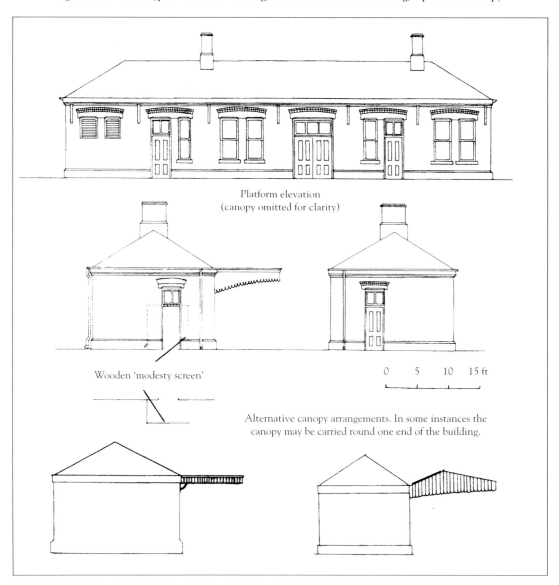

Platform elevation
(canopy omitted for clarity)

Wooden 'modesty screen'

0   5   10   15 ft

Alternative canopy arrangements. In some instances the canopy may be carried round one end of the building.

*Above* A modified Lima railcar enters 'Dimmock' station, modelled with a wealth of attractive detail in EM. *Tony Wright, courtesy Irwell Press*

*Below* Honeybourne station, as rebuilt with four platforms for the new Cheltenham-Birmingham line of 1906. Note the standard brick building with stone lintels, plinth, etc, cantilevered canopy, and paved platform surface. The bridges are also worthy of note in this and the previous photograph. The bridge at 'Dimmock' is built of steel girders with stone abutments and parapet, while at Honeybourne the rebuilding has resulted in a modified original stone/brick arch bridge abutting a more recent all-steel example. Bridges make useful scenic cut-offs or screens on the layout, as at 'Dimmock', and with a little imagination can be attractive modelling features in their own right. *Lens of Sutton*

By the early years of the present century, the main network had been established but the continued expansion of the railway and the construction of various 'cut-offs' provided the need and opportunity for new designs of building both as replacements for earlier structures on acquisitions and new facilities on the 'cut-offs'. The latter constructions led to stations appearing at points where there was little traffic potential, new stations being at best near mere hamlets. It must be assumed these were built more in hope than logical expectation.

Red brick was the order of the day for this era of standard design, with relief in blue brick, which was also used for plinth corners and window surrounds; corner bricks were 'bullnosed'. The buildings had hipped slate roofs with triangular glass skylights over the gents' toilets and a standard canopy cantilevered from the wall on the platform side. These canopies were on a steel frame – factory assembled from standard components – and had pitched roofs, clad at the front in iron sheeting and at the rear in glass. They rarely appeared other than on the platform side of the building. Figure 5 shows this style as seen at Lambourn.

**Figure 5: Lambourn station built in 1910 to what is often referred to as the 1902 standard design.**

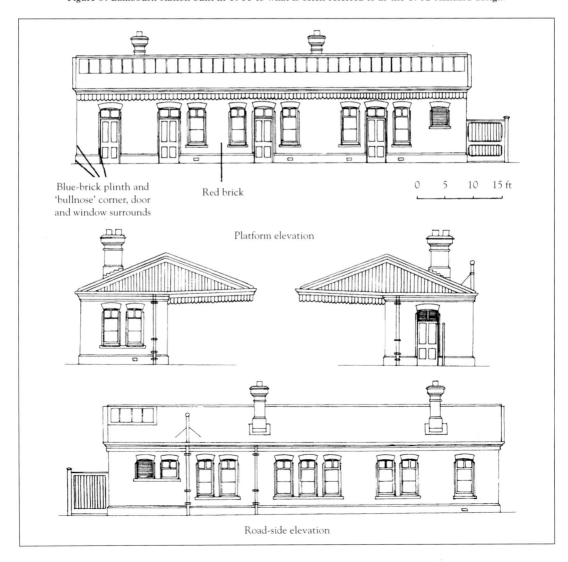

Blue-brick plinth and 'bullnose' corner, door and window surrounds

Red brick

0   5   10   15 ft

Platform elevation

Road-side elevation

Evesham station buildings are similar to those at Lambourn, this view showing at the near end the integral gents with its roof light. *Lens of Sutton*

Where these buildings were used as replacements, it was not unusual for earlier timberwork to be re-used. Some peculiarities did therefore exist, which gives an opportunity for some individuality to be given to a model. Tetbury station is a well-known and much photographed example of a standard station with a non-standard canopy.

Modellers of the British Railways period should be aware that is was not uncommon for these buildings to end their days without a canopy. This final appearance was not, in some cases, unpleasant, but when coupled with the general air of neglect and decay in the last years of many stations, it presented a very different picture altogether, symptomatic of the general malaise of a declining rail system – a very difficult challenge for the modeller to recreate.

There was little building or rebuilding after the start of the First World War, and where building did take place it was usually to individual design, major standardisation having ended. Buildings after this period were usually much more austere in appearance, ornate design and decoration having been lost to the previous age.

The principal exception to this lack of new building was in the construction of halts, which provided 'bus stop'-type facilities for small communities and were a direct result of the Great Western Railway's extensive use of railmotors, auto-trains and, later, railcars. These facilities continued to be built as this type of service expanded, and construction continued, albeit on a much more limited scale, under British Railways in the continued search for elusive traffic. Halt platforms were either a standard design of wooden frame with a platform surface of old sleepers (Figure 6), or a mound topped and finished in ash. Buildings were either simple wooden shelters, standard corrugated iron huts or standard 'Pagodas'. A simple wooden bench provided the only creature comfort. Concrete examples and tall 'bus shelter'-type back-and-roof-only versions also appeared latterly. Other features were usually fencing to the rear of the platform, a fenced walkway to the halt and oil lamps mounted on wooden posts. Exceptionally, such as at Foley Park Halt, a small wooden hut adjacent to the entrance was provided as a ticket collector's booth.

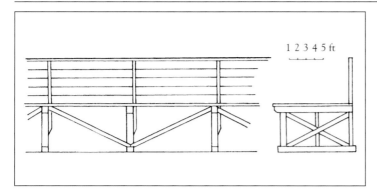

1 2 3 4 5 ft

*Top* Figure 6: Platform detail for a halt of timber construction, backed by post-and-wire fencing.

*Middle* Whitehall Halt built in 1933 on the Hemyock branch – a mound retained by a face of old sleepers and wooden edging. *Lens of Sutton*

*Bottom* The more substantial concrete-built halt at Golant, between Lostwithiel and Fowey. A rudimentary corrugated hut has been provided for passengers. *Lens of Sutton*

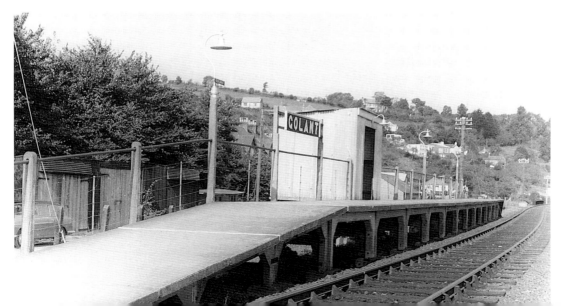

Having mentioned the accommodation at halts, it is prudent to mention at this juncture the standardised huts that found a variety of uses on the railway. The famous 'Pagoda' hut was introduced circa 1907 and was originally of concrete cladding on a steel frame. These could be seen in a variety of uses from waiting shelter to cycle shed. Later, the better-known types with corrugated steel cladding appeared. These were supplied in kit form by an outside contractor for assembly on site. They usually had a double door in the front centre, with a window on each side. However, there were various configurations with more doors, no window, etc, depending on usage, which could vary from platform shelter to lamp hut.

This building can provide a trap for modellers of West Country lines as they were also sold by contractors to other railways, notably the London & South Western. The presence of a 'Pagoda' does not therefore necessarily indicate GWR ownership. There were also other types of corrugated huts that found a variety of uses; Figures 7 and 8 illustrate these and the 'Pagodas'. Redundant 'Iron Mink' van bodies also found use as huts and sheds.

Before leaving the subject of passenger stations, it is also worth noting that there were many other types of station built by the Great Western Railway. There were wooden and stone versions of 'standard' buildings and individual designs, such as Castle Cary, for which a superb

*Right* Figure 7: Standard 'Pagoda' hut of corrugated iron.

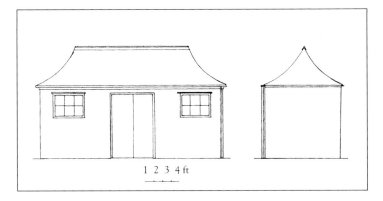

*Below* An LCGB railtour at Witney on the Fairford branch. Note the 'Pagoda' hut on the left, clearly used for storage rather than passenger accommodation. This example is embellished with decorative ridging and finials. *Ray Ruffell, Silver Link collection*

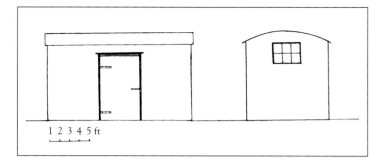

Figure 8: Iron hut found at many locations and used for purposes such as the storage of tools.

4mm scale kit is available, and Weston-super-Mare, which is a small-scale, individual architectural gem.

In the process of its expansion, the GWR took over other lines that already had buildings, and in the majority of instances, particularly on rural branch lines, these remained with little alteration. Some examples are illustrated. Of particular note were buildings by Arthur Pain for a number of small companies, perhaps the best-known examples of which being on the Culm Valley line in Devon. A Pain station building and shed are illustrated in Figure 9.

# Goods facilities

Goods facilities varied enormously, dependent upon the anticipated usage and traffic handled at a particular location. Goods shed were usually designed to match, or at least complement, the architecture of the station. Classical or even ecclesiastical styles were not unknown, and some, such as at Newbury, shared the Brunellian designs of the Berks & Hants line, echoing the station with its style of brickwork and semi-circular arches over the windows in yellow brick; even the wooden lean-to echoed the curved window designs.

Goods sheds could be of stone, brick or timber construction and typically comprised a single-track through road, the end walls of the shed having arched entrance/exits for the railway wagons, a central platform for loading and unloading and, on the road side, entrance through large sliding doors for road vehicles. The platform was usually wooden, but brick and stone were not unheard of.

The later standard red brick station buildings were accompanied by a similar style of goods sheds, which also used standard manufactured doors and windows. At the other end of the scale, the minimum goods shed facility provided might consist only of a small lock-up building without wagon access, and an accompanying loading bank.

Cattle loading facilities – pens, docks, or whatever nomenclature you wish – were usually found at most stations and may indeed have been the only structure provided to handle freight. A drawing of a standard GWR design (Figure 10) is included. The 2mm or 4mm scale modeller wanting anything but basic facilities and not wanting to scratch-build can do little better than utilise the Ratio models.

Goods sheds were likely to be modified and extended or even rebuilt if traffic needs demanded. Additional lean-to sheds and offices annexed to the main goods sheds are one example, and additional space created by the use of various small huts and cabins often of the standard designs is another. Small goods warehouses with a timber frame and asbestos sheet cladding began to appear from the mid-1930s to expand facilities. A drawing of a typical one of these structures is included (Figure 11).

The average small to medium goods yard may also have included a weighbridge and stables. The GWR employed more than 20,000 horses before 1914, mainly on road haulage; a drawing of some typical stables is included (Figure 12). An excellent 4mm scale Pooley weighbridge and hut is available from Coopercraft, as is a platelayers' hut of wooden construction with brick chimney. The weighbridge may well have had a standard corrugated iron or 'Pagoda' hut as the office, and substituting these would increase variety.

Figure 9: Arthur Pain designed buildings to a similar design for several small railways. Above is a plan and side elevation of a typical boarded building, while the end elevation is a brick building with a wooden frame, such as at Hemyock. The lower drawings show a boarded 'barn'-type Pain goods shed.

*Above* The wooden goods shed with lean-to office on Ken Cottle's Scale 7 'Weston Green' layout. *Tony Wright*

*Below* Figure 10: Cattle dock.

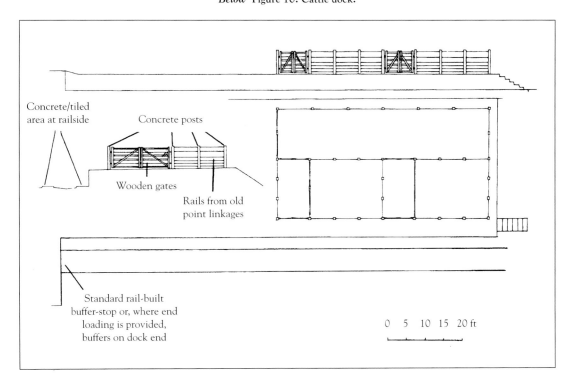

Concrete/tiled area at railside

Concrete posts

Wooden gates

Rails from old point linkages

Standard rail-built buffer-stop or, where end loading is provided, buffers on dock end

0   5   10  15  20 ft

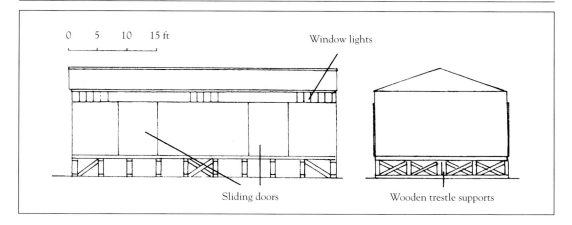

0   5   10   15 ft

Window lights

Sliding doors

Wooden trestle supports

*Above* Figure 11: A sheet-and-timber warehouse as mentioned in the text. Sizes varied to suit the location.

*Right* Figure 12: Typical GWR-style stables to be found at any reasonably sized station or goods facility. Larger and smaller versions were built to serve local needs.

0 1 2 3 4 ft

*Below* The unroofed lattice girder footbridge at Kingham. *Lens of Sutton*

*Above* Ledbury station footbridge, of plate girder construction with a valanced roof, modelled in 4mm scale. This was a prize-winner at Scaleforum '98. *Tony Wright*

*Below* The standard type of pre-cast concrete footbridge as illustrated in *The Great Western Railway Magazine* of May 1936.

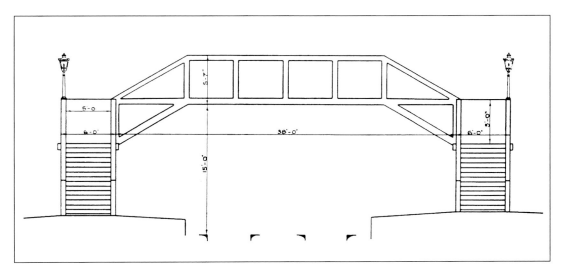

It is generally accepted that footbridges on the GWR took their well-known form from the 1880s. The GWR was a keen user of footbridges, which basically comprise two types, the lattice girder and plate girder; examples of both are illustrated. There were, of course, many other varieties of footbridge, and kits have been available for both 'standard' types in 2mm and 4mm scales.

# Engine sheds

The GWR had a wide variety of engine sheds, many of the smaller examples being unique to their particular location and well-known to modellers, such as the wooden structure at Fairford, Ashburton's stone shed and Tetbury's brick-built one. The GWR inherited many sheds from the South Wales railways, and also had its own standard designs for larger structures.

The earliest sheds were of timber construction, but, as the company became more established, most were later replaced with brick-built types. Several of the earliest brick structures consisted of a straight-road shed with the turntable immediately outside, but separate, as at Basingstoke. Other major sheds consisted of a turntable shed alone or one connected to a straight-road shed or another turntable shed.

Typical shed layouts from various locations are shown in Figure 13.

The Dean 'Northlight' sheds, straight-road facilities built in the latter part of the 19th century, became quite widespread and this type of shed often also had repair shops and other accommodation alongside. Similar roof patterns also appeared on turntable sheds built at this period, such as that at Croes Newydd.

Churchward's standardisation drive also applied to running sheds. His first design in 1906 was at Old Oak Common, which comprised four large turntable sheds under a common roof. Other turntable sheds were constructed in this style but not of such size, accommodating only one or two tables. The 'Northlight' roof was abandoned by Churchward in favour of conventional pitched roofs for all types of shed. His straight-road sheds were also designed to enable further bays to be added.

**A branch line timber-built engine shed, with wooden coaling stage and water tower, on Mike Corps's TT 'West Harptree' layout.** *Tony Wright, courtesy British Railway Modelling*

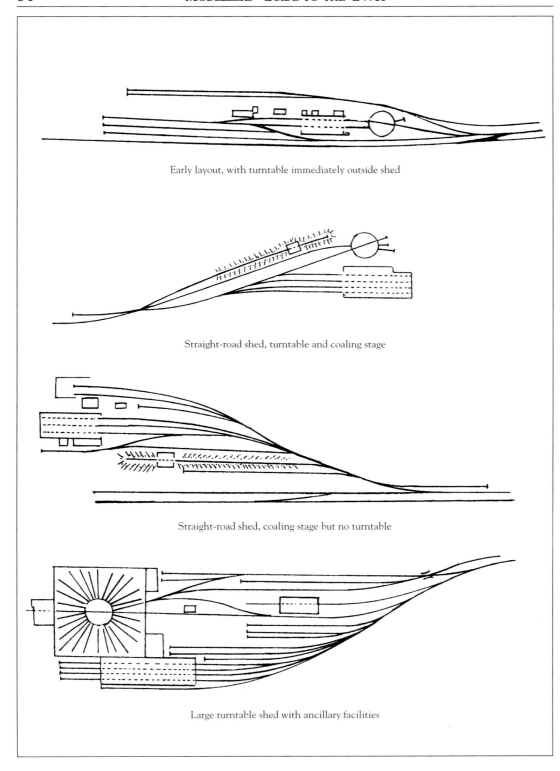

Early layout, with turntable immediately outside shed

Straight-road shed, turntable and coaling stage

Straight-road shed, coaling stage but no turntable

Large turntable shed with ancillary facilities

Figure 13: Typical GWR engine shed layouts.

A typical small stone-built engine shed with water tank combined, built in O gauge by Allan Downes. *Tony Wright*

A much larger locomotive facility modelled in OO gauge on **Ted Kanas's** system. The elevated coaling stage with water tank above is a typical feature of such main-line installations. *Tony Wright, courtesy Irwell Press*

On larger layouts or in the smaller gauges, accommodation for coaches should not be overlooked. This model carriage shed, constructed in plastic, is on Leo McCarthy's N gauge 'Penny Forum' layout. In reality such sheds turned up at surprising locations, including branch termini, and were usually built from local materials, wood not being uncommon. *Tony Wright*

Several new straight-road sheds were built, but inevitably the First World War halted construction and rebuilding, as did the post-war economic climate. However, the Government's 1929 Loans and Guarantees Act enabled the replacement and updating of facilities absorbed at the Grouping and the construction of new sheds, of the straight-road variety, both as replacements for absorbed sheds in South Wales and older facilities in England.

The Second World War resulted in the provision of increased facilities, in particular lifting shops at several locations, in response to wartime pressures for further types of repair to be undertaken at running sheds, thus minimising time out of traffic.

Nationalisation did not stop development and new sheds were built, notably at Southall; Pwllheli received a new steel-framed building as late as 1958. Dieselisation brought further changes, not least the rapid closure of many sheds, the last to operate steam on the Western Region being Weymouth. A few sheds survived to be adapted for diesel use.

## Colour schemes

The Great Western Railway had its own distinct colour schemes for buildings, signs, lineside equipment, lamp posts, etc, which helped to establish the corporate identity of the railway.

Two principal colour schemes were used on these various structures, either light and dark stone, or maroon, brown and white. The former, more common colours are available in the proprietary model paint ranges, although it is worth noting that there would be some variation in these colours as they were mixed on site; furthermore, weathering would affect the colouring. The GWR did not paint its buildings chocolate and cream, although BR repaints did occur in these colours. The maroon brown was a colour that weathered well and in particularly exposed and vulnerable locations was sometimes used instead of dark stone. It thus occurs more commonly on signal boxes and raised areas, such as door panelling or wooden doorsteps subject to high levels of wear and abuse, although the latter practice seems to have been more common in the early period of the company.

The basic colour scheme for buildings was as follows:

**Stone or brick buildings:** Goods sheds, warehouses, station buildings, signal boxes, etc. *Light stone* Door frames, window-sills and mullions, barge-boards and recessed door panels, decorative ironwork on ridge of roof. *Dark stone* Door frames and raised door panels, external wooden features, wooden plinths, gutters and drainpipes. *White* Window sashes, casements and glazing bars.

**Timber buildings:** Goods sheds, station buildings, signal boxes, etc. *Light stone* Recessed door panels, barge-boards and walls. *Dark stone* Raised door panels, door jambs, window frames and sills, building frame, gutters and drainpipes. *White* Window sashes, casements and glazing bars.

**'Pagodas' and other corrugated huts:** *Black* Roofs. *Light stone* Main shell of building. *Dark stone* Doors. *White* Window frames.

**Awnings and canopies:** *Light stone* Valancing, plain canopy supports. *Dark stone* Horizontal woodwork, decoration on supports, steel framing of canopies. NB Before the Grouping, valances were often light/dark stone on alternate planks.

**Other features:** *Lamps* Light stone with decoration where provided, picked out in dark stone and black, ironwork round lamphead. *Poster boards* Black with light stone edging. *Cast signs and nameboards* Black with white lettering, light stone posts and surrounds.

Notices and signage make for an entertaining and challenging modelling project. The first was photographed at Barmouth as recently as 1970, the second reminds us of one of the GWR's principal constituent companies, while the third photograph shows a range of finely restored platform signs at Toddington station. *Ray Ruffell, Silver Link collection (2)/Will Adams*

# 8
# SIGNALLING AND
# THE PERMANENT WAY

This chapter takes a brief look at the development of signalling practice, signal boxes and trackwork on the Great Western Railway, and drawings and illustrations are included to show typical situations. Additionally there are some track layouts to show representative signalling arrangements. Hopefully these will be helpful to the modeller and, in conjunction with the text, will enable layouts to be signalled in something approaching an authentic manner. The subject of signalling is complex and inevitably only the broadest outline of the Great Western Railway's signalling practice can be given.

## Signalling

Brunel – who else? – introduced the first mechanical signalling on the Great Western Railway in 1840; this was the well-known 'disc and crossbar' signal (see page 11). Hitherto, signalling had relied upon patrolling 'constables' giving hand signals on a 'time elapsed' basis; this gave no protection from trains running into each other, as the system only ensured that a certain period of time had elapsed between trains passing a given point, not the distance that the last train had travelled.

Brunel's 'disc and crossbar' was the first signalling to indicate clearly 'stop' and 'go'. The disc, viewed face-on, indicated 'all right', and beneath, at 90 degrees to it, was the crossbar, which, when turned to face the oncoming train, indicated danger. It is interesting to note that on these early signals it was the shape of the signal, the disc or crossbar, rather than the colour that gave the signal. With the disc and bar being at 90 degrees to each other on the post, the mechanical arrangement was simply a matter of

turning one or other to face the oncoming train, the other signal automatically being turned away. Several variations of this type of signal were developed, but they were largely superseded by the late 1880s, although odd examples remained after this date.

The successor was the archetypal Great Western signal, the lower quadrant with the steeply inclined clear, or 'off', position and wide arms mounted, invariably, on a tapered, square wooden post capped with a ball-and-spike finial. These signals, still with lower-quadrant arms of various designs and types, lasted until the late 1960s. The railway companies joining with the Great Western Railway at the 1923 Grouping had their own signalling, often bought in from manufacturers such as Saxby & Farmer or Mackenzie & Holland. However, the GWR quickly set about replacing these varied installations with its own standard product.

Shortage of suitable timber during the Second World War led the GWR to develop tubular steel posts for signals, and these became the standard for replacements and were quite widespread by the early 1960s, some examples still being extant. It should also be noted that while the Great Western Railway had far more standardised signals than other companies after the Grouping, it did have a few oddities, including a lattice-post specimen.

The basic premise of the semaphore signalling system used by the Great Western –and all the other major companies – from the late 19th century onwards was, unlike the early days, the control of trains according to the distance between them, the aim being to ensure an adequate distance between trains approaching or crossing each other's path and between following trains. This became known as the 'block' system,

*Right* A 1930s illustration of common forms of GWR lower-quadrant signals, including the basic Stop signal – used as Home or Starter – and the Distant. The others allow trains to reverse or shunt within a block section, while the ringed arm denotes one controlling a siding, distinguishing it visually from a main running line signal.

*Left* A bracket signal controlling a junction, scratch-built by Eric Harrison and the late Geoff Powell in 7mm scale. The posts are wooden and tapered, topped by ball-and-spike finials, while the signal arms are painted wood (red with a white stripe for a Stop signal) with separate cast iron pivot and spectacle housings. Note also the corrugated iron lamp hut, a safe fireproof environment for the filling of signal lamps with oil. *Tony Wright*

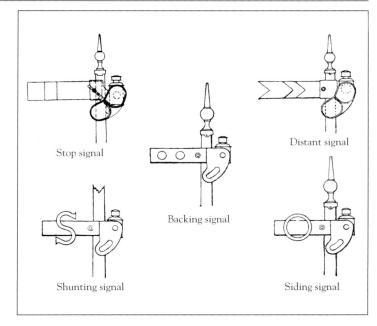

Stop signal

Distant signal

Backing signal

Shunting signal

Siding signal

*Below* The rear of a similar bracket signal, with one arm 'off' to allow the railcar to take the left-hand divergence. The rear of these wooden arms are white with a black stripe. Note also the standard GWR wooden signal box with hipped roof and ventilators (see Figure 15) on the Wolverhampton MRC's 'Woden Road' layout. *Tony Wright*

*Above left* Later signals were mounted on tubular steel posts and had enamelled metal arms, as this bracket example at Stroud, photographed in 1970. The white diamond indicates that the line is track-circuited, which means that the presence of the train is indicated by a light on the signal box track diagram. *Will Adams*

*Above right* Tubular steel Stop signals preserved on the Severn Valley Railway at Kidderminster. On the nearer one the 'ground signal' – a white-and-red-striped enamel disc that rotates 45 degrees anticlockwise to signal shunting movements, and is normally located at track level – is mounted on the post to aid visibility. The far signal has a route indicator, whereby a single arm can control access to a number of routes by means of stencilled slides that appear in the upper portion of the frame when the appropriate lever is pulled. *Tony Wright*

whereby the railway line is divided into sections known as blocks. Normally, not more than one train is allowed on each running line in a block at one time. The signal box for each block section controls the entrance and exit of trains by means of signals. Although there are a wide variety of signal configurations and several types of special purpose signals, it is convenient for ordinary purposes to identify the three fundamental types, Distant, Home and Starting.

The Distant signal is the first signal to be encountered, and lets the driver know whether the way ahead is clear. It is a warning signal, and is the only signal that can be passed when at 'danger', ie the 'on' position. Although the signal can be passed, the train must be slowed down as the Distant in this position indicates that the next Stop signal, some 800 yards or so ahead, is likely to be at danger. Where the Distant is 'off', the train can proceed normally. A 'fixed' (non-operational) Distant may appear at the approach to bay platforms, termini, speed-restricted junctions or on branch lines where there is a 15mph speed restriction. These signals are usually modified with a fixed arm and spectacle plate and a lamp fixed to the post permanently showing amber.

On occasions, where signal boxes are close together and there is insufficient distance to locate a Distant far enough in advance of its accompanying Stop signal, it is placed on the same post as the Starting signal for the previous block section. This situation gives rise to the familiar two-arm Home and Distant signal. In some cases, particularly on entering through stations, one distant signal may be controlled by more than one box.

The second signal reached in the section is the Home signal, the purpose of which is to stop trains before entering the section or to stop them before reaching junctions, level crossings, passing loops, etc, within the section. Outer and inner Home signals are used for acceptance purposes – by placing an outer Home a quarter of a mile before the inner Home, once a train has passed the inner Home a second train can be accepted as far as the outer.

The third signal is the Starting signal, and this controls the entry of the train into the next block section. This signal is located so that any train movements within the section, such as shunting, can be carried out without the Starting signal being passed. In instances where this is not possible and there is pointwork close to the Starting signal, an advanced Starting signal is positioned ahead of it.

Ground signals add another important visual touch of authenticity. These are specifically intended to control train movements over points and crossovers to, from or between sidings, etc, usually in a trailing direction and generally not for use over points used by passenger trains. The earliest form of ground signal on the Great Western Railway was contemporary with the 'disc and crossbar' mentioned earlier, and was similarly arranged to turn a disc through 90 degrees, indicating 'stop' or 'go' over points. Further development came with the linking of point control to lever frames when a signal combining a lamp and crossbar was introduced, which worked with the action of the point. Subsequently this evolved into merely a lamp that turned through 90 degrees and was set down at rail level. It had red and green lamp glasses surrounded by a red rectangle and green circle respectively.

Independent signals indicating the settings of points were the next development. These were controlled from the signal box and were worked separately from the point lever. The earlier examples were a simple miniature semaphore just above rail level with a lamp behind for night-time identification through coloured lenses at one end of the arm, much the same as in a normal semaphore signal.

The next stage in the development of ground signals was the provision of a white 'three-quarter length' disc with the arm enamelled red across it and a continuance of the arrangement of the spectacle plate/lamps. This in turn evolved into the full disc, such signals being known throughout the GWR as 'dummies'.

A number of electrically operated colour light signals also appeared on the Great Western Railway, but it should be said at the outset that these were a far cry from what we now understand colour light signals to be. They did not have the multi-aspect, track control link of contemporary modern signals, but merely echoed the traditional red/green Stop and amber/green Distant aspects of semaphore signals, and were worked in accordance with the established block regulations. They are often referred to as searchlight signals and had a very distinctive appearance with a single small-diameter round lamphood in the centre of a larger round disc. Later examples, introduced late in the Second World War, had tubular steel posts, and even later examples had a different arrangement of lamps, more like the modern types. The painting scheme for these signals is worth mentioning. The base, hood and background were painted black, as were the ladders, while the post and rear of the lamps were aluminium. The finials, which continued to be provided on colour light signal posts, were either red or yellow, depending on whether the signal was a Stop or Distant.

The 'banner repeater' was another electrically operated signal, being used when, for example, a bridge impaired the view of a signal or where the curve of the track was so sharp that the signal ahead could not be seen easily by the driver of an oncoming train. The repeater was placed in such a position that the driver could easily see it, but it did not in itself constitute a signal; it was merely a back-lit black bar that rotated to mirror the position of the obscured signal. Figure 14 shows a typical example, although single posts could have two repeaters for, perhaps, home and distant signals.

The well-known GWR Automatic Train Control system (ATC) deserves a mention under the heading of signalling. It was first tried in 1906 on the Fairford branch, and by 1931 all main lines had been equipped with this safety device. It was essentially an electrical contact operation, a shoe beneath the locomotive making contact with a ramp between the rails. The ramps varied in length between 40 and 60 feet and were positioned 400 yards to the rear of a Distant signal. When a locomotive passed over the ramp when the Distant was 'on', the ramp pushed up a contact shoe beneath the loco, initiating a brake application and sounding a siren. The driver, on hearing the warning, bypassed the automatic process and took charge

of events himself, braking as he would normally. If he did not, the train would stop automatically. Where the signal was 'off', an electromagnet within the ramp was energised; the ramp still raised the contact shoe, but the energised magnet affected a receiver in the shoe that overrode the initiation of the brake application, and a different signal, a bell, indicating 'all clear', was sounded. It was thus a 'fail-safe' system – if the current failed, an automatic brake application was initiated.

# Signal boxes

Signal boxes on the Great Western Railway came in a variety of shapes and styles, many inherited from absorbed railways or from constituent companies at the Grouping. The Great Western Railway itself produced several designs, and while reference is often made to standard types, it is difficult to establish exactly what a standard design was, although it must be admitted that there were, as with stations and other buildings discussed in Chapter 6, clear architectural families.

All-timber boxes were most common before 1900, but were also built much later. Brick-built boxes became the norm in the 20th century until the 1930s, when concrete block construction was introduced. The all-brick designs were neat structures with hipped roofs and characteristic roof vents. The locking-room window and door openings were arched in blue brick, which also adorned the corners. They were smooth surfaced with no other decoration. Later versions of these boxes had gable ends rather than hipped roofs but were otherwise similar.

There is ample scope for detailing model signal boxes, particularly the interiors, and detailing packs are available in 4mm and 7mm scales from Springside Models. Careful painting of the interior will be well rewarded. The following colours were used by the Great Western for levers:

Distant signals: green or yellow (green pre-1920)
Stop signals and ground signals: red
Points: black
Locking bolt levers: blue
Ground frame locking levers: brown

**Figure 14: A Sykes banner repeater.**

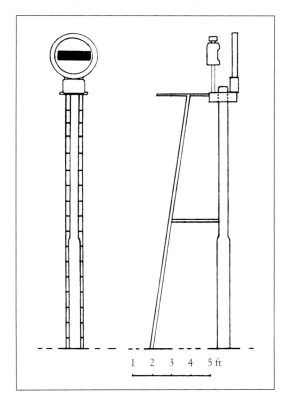

1   2   3   4   5 ft

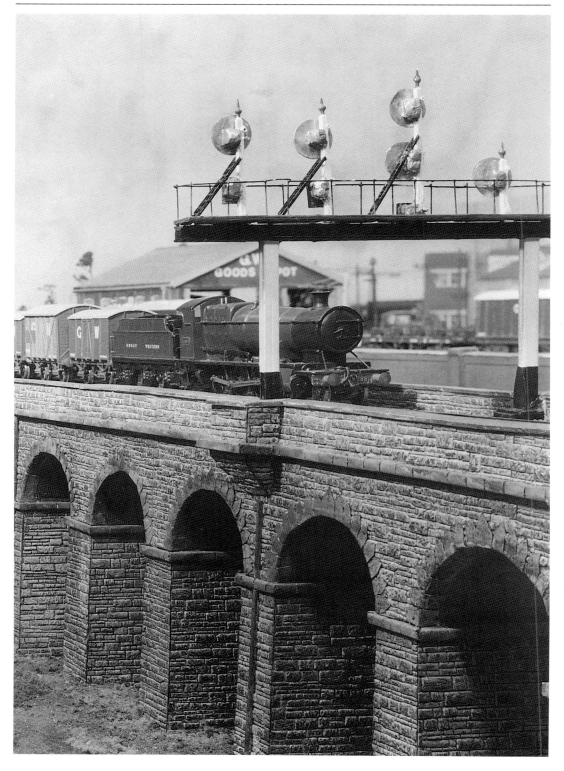

GWR 'target' colour light signals on the OO 'Whitchurch Road' layout of the Cardiff (Whitchurch) MES. *Tony Wright*

The interior of the box, besides the levers, consisted of a track diagram hung over the instrument shelf above the lever frame. A tall desk was provided, usually against the opposite wall, and a cupboard that was black with cream doors. A small table and chair and simple bench were also provided, together with a clock and, of course, a stove. Running water was not usually provided! Signal box interiors were kept very clean and the metalwork well polished. The signalman usually used a cloth to hold the polished lever handles so that his sweaty hands would not dull the shine. Details of the exterior painting scheme for signal boxes are included in Chapter 6 under details of the painting schemes for buildings.

*Opposite page and above* As well as its own 'standard' designs, the GWR inherited different styles of signal boxes from its constituent companies. These three are all Cambrian Railways examples, Barmouth South, Barmouth North and Llwyngwril. There was normally an often elaborate telegraph pole adjacent to a signal box, carrying the various telephone and telegraph lines. Note the Stop and Distant signal protecting the level crossing at Barmouth South; the Distant will be that of North Box, and there is also a subsidiary 'shunt ahead' signal, allowing limited movement forward into North's section. Coal bunkers and lamp huts are other common features in the vicinity of a signal box. While the Barmouth boxes are entirely glazed above, Llwyngwril has fewer and smaller windows, and shows signs of having been extended in a basic yet practical manner at the far end! *All Ray Ruffell, Silver Link collection*

*Below* The brick-built box at Williton on the West Somerset Railway. Unlike those of many other companies, the GWR generally included the words 'Signal Box' on the name plate. *Ray Ruffell, Silver Link collection*

Brick construction, hipped roof

Wooden construction, hipped roof

Gable-ended, side and rear views showing windows to the rear.
Sometimes there were rear windows at one end only,
or no windows at the back at all, depending on location.

0    5    10 ft

Figure 15: The 'standard' GWR signal box design.

Variations on the 'standard' GWR signal box. The quaint brick-based crossing box at Frampton Mansell on the Stroud-Swindon line has a gable-ended roof and a brace of corrugated iron huts. The much larger box at Towyn is also gable-ended and of all-timber construction, as seen in Figure 15; note the automatic single-line tablet catching apparatus at the far end, and the platform at the near end for the tablet exchange to be done manually. *Will Adams/Ray Ruffell, Silver Link collection*

*Above*  The standard hip-roofed pattern of box at Dawlish, but lack of room has led to a narrow base, with the operating floor projecting over the platform, a useful dodge for the space-restricted modeller! *Ray Ruffell, Silver Link collection*

*Below*  The more recent-looking hip-roofed box at Penzance. Note that this style had an internal staircase. *Ray Ruffell, Silver Link collection*

*Above* To reflect the modernisation of former GWR lines, the modeller might like to try something a little different, like this replacement box at Whitland, possibly dating from the rebuilding of the station in 1958. Certainly lacking the charm of more traditional structures, it controls the barrier crossing, colour light signals on the main line, and semaphore signals on the Pembroke branch. *Ray Ruffell, Silver Link collection*

*Below* The delightful stone-based signal box at Willow on Allan Downes's O gauge layout. *Tony Wright*

# Trackwork

This section principally describes the construction of Brunel's broad gauge trackwork, the 'baulk road', which together with the accompanying drawing (Figure 16) should indicate to the modeller the principles involved. There are no readily available components for broad gauge track, although specialist societies have arranged for products to be available to their members. Readers wishing to model the broad gauge are referred to the Broad Gauge Model Railway Society, the secretary of which is listed in Appendix 1. Additionally there have been articles in the model railway press from time to time on broad gauge matters.

The 'baulk road' gets its name from the fact that broad gauge trackwork was constructed of light section rail fixed to continuous longitudinal wooden timbers (baulks), which were held in gauge by intermittent cross pieces of smaller-section timber. Initially the cross pieces were at 15-foot intervals, and were fixed

to piles driven into the ground. This was not successful and later the piles were cut and the cross pieces spaced at 8-foot intervals. The rail used in this type of trackwork was not of the more commonly known pattern but 'bridge' rail. In section it was literally arched like a bridge, although the exact shape varied as the size of rail increased to meet the loads of heavier locomotives and stock.

'Narrow' (standard) gauge trackwork on the Great Western Railway was invariably built in the conventional style with timber sleepers spaced at intervals of 2ft 7in, or 2ft 4in at rail joints. Bullhead trackwork was the norm until the late 1950s when much main-line trackwork was replaced by flat bottom rail.

The choice of model railway trackwork will be governed to a large extent by the gauge modelled and the inclination of the modeller, who may or may not wish to build his own. The details of 4mm trackwork construction are regularly described in the model press and are beyond the scope of this book. However, two points are

Figure 16: The basic construction of 'baulk road' trackwork.

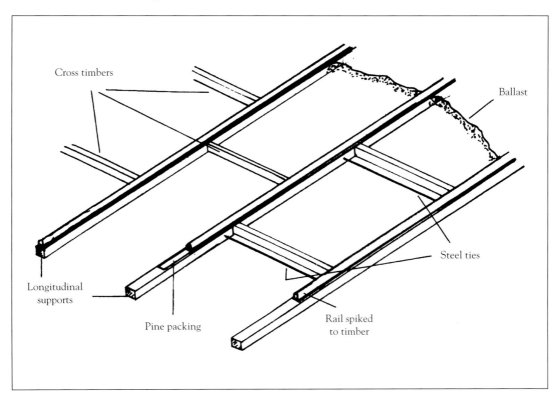

Cross timbers

Ballast

Steel ties

Longitudinal supports

Pine packing

Rail spiked to timber

worth mentioning for those building their own trackwork: the Great Western Railway used two-bolt chairs and generally used short check rails usually spanning only four sleepers.

Trackwork terminology is often confusing to the modeller, so Figure 18 is included to indicate the common terminology used in reference to pointwork.

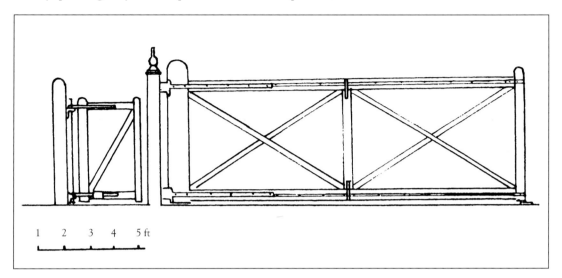

*Above* Figure 17: Level crossing gate and foot crossing gate. Gates varied in size depending on the location, the number of tracks spanned, the road width, etc, but construction, using standard ironwork, was similar.

*Below* Figure 18: Pointwork terminology.

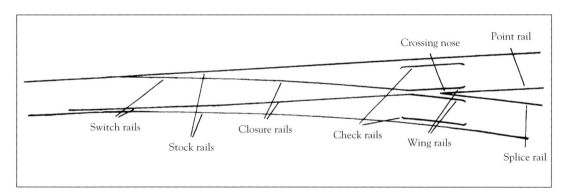

# 9
# ROAD VEHICLES

Railways were great users of road vehicles and the Great Western Railway was certainly no exception. Its earliest road vehicles were horse-drawn, a mode of traction that lasted into the immediate post-Second World War period.

Vast numbers of horses were used by the GWR. These animals required caring for and feeding, and the railway had a horse hospital at West Ealing and a huge store for provender at Didcot. Horse-drawn vehicles came in a great variety of sizes and types, from small two-wheeled carts and parcel vans drawn by single horses to huge four-horse wagons.

Although it is often assumed that railway bus services were introduced as a result of competition from road services, many of the railway companies, including the Great Western, operated horse-drawn 'omnibuses' well before the turn of the 20th century. Some of these vehicles mirrored the contemporary practice of similar non-railway vehicles, having a top deck open to the elements with an outside staircase leading to seats literally on the roof.

Construction of the majority of horse-drawn vehicles was undertaken at Swindon Works. Surprisingly, new designs of parcel delivery van, with pneumatic tyres and electric lighting, were still being produced in the late 1930s.

There are a number of horse-drawn vehicles produced in the popular modelling scales, but none of specific GWR vehicles. However, it is a comparatively simple task to modify these vehicles to GWR types, particularly those made in plastic. Military modelling books and magazines often contain details of the construction and conversion of vehicles of all types, and here the railway modeller may well learn to his advantage from the expertise of the military modeller. A great many drawings of GWR road vehicles and, most usefully, photographs appear in *Road Vehicles of the Great Western Railway* and *Great Western Road Vehicle Appendix* by Philip J. Kelley; originally published by OPC, a new edition of the former has recently been published by Ian Allan. Additionally, drawings have appeared occasionally in the model press, and reference to the Leleux Index of Model Railway Drawings may well prove useful.

By contrast, there are quite a few authentic models of GWR motor road vehicles available, often in kit form, for the most popular scales. The GWR experimented with the use of steam lorries in the early years of the 20th century, and before the outbreak of the First World War was operating a growing number of motor road vehicles, steam-powered, petrol-driven and even battery-electric.

The Great War really brought forward dramatically the development and use of motor road vehicles, and the ready availability of cheap war surplus vehicles no doubt helped. Before the war, parcels vans used the Mills-Daimler chassis; Swindon-built bodies were favoured, although various other vehicles were also used. The first motor parcels vans were Wolseley.

After the war, a large number of ex-WD vehicles became available, notable among which were 3½-ton AECs, for which the GWR built alternative bodies – charabancs for summer, lorries in winter.

Among the other varied vehicles used in the inter-war years and for which kits have been available are 30cwt Thornycrofts. Many of the 1927 forward-control Thornycrofts incorporated an ingenious three-quarter sliding tilt; this was a rigid body the top and sides of which could be slid forwards over the cab to enable easy loading of the flat bed, the roof and sides being slid back

An AEC 3½-ton solid-tyred lorry, Fleet No 184, photographed at Paddington shortly after delivery to the GWR in 1921. This was one of the first vehicles purchased from the War Department. *Both Philip J. Kelley collection*

*Above* 30cwt D-type Burford forward-control flat lorry No 574, photographed at Swindon Works on 22 November 1923. The livery is chocolate brown and cream, and the engine cover and bonnet are lined out. *Philip J. Kelley collection*

*Below* A 4-ton Thornycroft PB forward-control lorry, Fleet No 1361, its flat body fitted with high sides and a solid removable tilt (top cover). *Philip J. Kelley collection*

when loading was complete. Morris, Bedford and AEC developments were also used. 1927 was also significant in heralding the introduction of pneumatic tyres.

Such was the growth in the use of motor transport by the GWR that repair shops were constructed at Slough in 1926. Many special vehicles were developed to suit particular traffic needs, such as cattle wagons and tipping wagons. There was also a considerable amount of joint development between the railway companies and motor vehicle manufacturers, and, indeed, between the railway companies themselves in the operation of 'cartage' services, several joint services being established.

Extensive use was made of agricultural tractors, particularly Fordsons, for hauling special trailers. Battery-electric traction, first tried in 1906 as a result of American influence, was continued after the First World War in larger vehicles for local deliveries, particularly in London. Large 2-ton

motor parcels vans were being delivered up to the advent of nationalisation.

The GWR seems to have had a particularly fruitful business relationship with Thornycroft, especially in the 1920s and early 1930s, a wide variety of Thornycroft-based vehicles being used. The GWR did, however, require a great variety of road transport and the products of other companies were also utilised. The use of steam-powered vehicles continued, Foden Steam Wagons being purchased as late as 1929 for heavy haulage.

Early innovation in the use of road transport came with the introduction of a scheme of contract hire whereby vans were hired out for the exclusive use of the hiring company. A number of major companies took part in the scheme, amongst them Cadbury, Macfarlane Lang and Rowntree.

Experiments took place in 1931 with the use of a mechanical tractor and demountable trailer

The body of this Thornycroft 30cwt A1 chassis, Fleet No 976, was built at Swindon, but is shown here adapted for contract hire to Macfarlane, Lang & Co. The photograph was taken at Redruth in January 1928; note the electric head and side lights in addition to the oil side lamps, and the pneumatic tyres. The livery is standard GWR, with Macfarlane, Lang's green side boards. *Philip J. Kelley collection*

arrangement. Horses, as noted earlier, lasted well and were the ideal power for haulage of light loads over short distances, being the most economic and convenient for this type of haulage. However, horses were comparatively slow and afforded only limited haulage capacity. The GWR therefore sought the ideal answer in the form of a 'mechanical horse'. Various types of vehicles were tested, including the Knox tractor/trailer from the USA. Trailers were developed to be easily detachable and capable of being coupled to the tractor with maximum ease, the driver not even having to leave his cab. Initially, many of the early trailers used were converted from horse-drawn flat vehicles, but ultimately a large fleet of trailers was built for general use, either flat or covered, with specially designed examples for carrying cattle or other specific goods.

In 1934 the Scammell patent coupling was adopted by the 'Big Four' railway companies as standard for 'mechanical horse' and trailer couplings. By agreement with the company, the railways were able to use this on other types of vehicle than Scammells.

The three-wheel 'mechanical horse' system was now firmly established as part of the railway scene until the decimation of general goods services in the 1960s. Its advantages, other than speed and haulage capacity, lay in its manoeuvrability and versatility; trailers could be left for loading or unloading while the tractor unit left the site to continue other duties.

In addition to the well-known three-wheel 'mechanical horse', a variety of four-wheel tractor units were also developed from other commercial vehicles such as Morris and Thornycroft. These vehicles were intended for heavier loads and were more akin to the modern articulated lorry than the speedy, highly mobile mechanical horse, intended for local deliveries.

The GWR was a pioneer of railway-operated bus services, its first starting in 1903 between Helston and The Lizard in Cornwall. This service was started as a direct result of the estimated high cost of constructing a rail link between the two locations. Bus services were quickly developed, not only by the GWR but also by most other railway companies. Services were initially intended to feed towns not connected to the rail network rather than connecting locations already served by rail. However, it was soon realised that direct services generated traffic and consequently many were introduced, often because the route taken was more direct than that of the railway and therefore quicker!

A 6-ton Scammell Mechanical Horse, Fleet No 2737, with trailer No T228. Note that the tarpaulin also bears the trailer number. *Philip J. Kelley collection*

A GWR Maudsley bus has brought passengers to 'Dimmock' station – an authentic Great Western branch line scene. *Tony Wright, courtesy Irwell Press*

The rapid growth in the use of motor transport after the First World War was also apparent in bus services. Many small private bus enterprises were established and competition was acute. As a consequence, many of the smaller companies expanded and acquired other companies in the process. The result was that the GWR entered into agreements with several operators such as Crossville for the provision of services. Ultimately, this process led in 1933 to the end of independent GWR bus operation.

Of the buses themselves, the earliest examples showed a distinct likeness to horse-drawn vehicles; the wagonettes used between Helston and The Lizard, for example, showed a clear lineage. The GWR had, as noted earlier, used horse-drawn omnibuses itself.

Various body styles were tried with varying results, some double, some single deck, and many open charabancs. In the early days of motor buses, the GWR favoured the Milnes-Daimler chassis, but shortage of suitable vehicles meant a number of types had to be used, including some rather unsuccessful 20hp steam-powered vehicles.

After the First World War, the situation was somewhat different, many ex-WD vehicles initially being available. Particularly noteworthy among these was the AEC chassis already mentioned, which had removable bus bodies for summer use and wagon bodies for haulage use in winter. As with goods vehicles, many bus bodies were built at Swindon, while Burford, Thornycroft, AEC, Guy and Maudsley all provided the basis of vehicles for the fleet. The vast majority of vehicles were single-deckers.

Two interesting points arise from the development of bus services. First, the GWR developed corrugated iron buildings as local garages, often capable of housing only one vehicle. Second, the erstwhile and ever enterprising Publicity Department decorated buses with details and posters of areas such as the Cornish Riviera, filled the inside with handbills and publicity material and sent them on long publicity tours, as far away as the North of Scotland, to publicise the railway and, hopefully, generate traffic.

As with the goods vehicles, there have been some models available in kit form. In most notably 2mm, 4mm and 7mm scales there have been cast metal kits of Thornycroft vehicles available, and in 4mm scale there is an excellent plastic kit of a Maudsley ML3.

# Road vehicle liveries

Road vehicle liveries usually involved variations on the theme of chocolate and cream with varying types of lettering used, including, from the mid-1930s, the 'shirt button' monogram and, of course, on van sides plenty of space to display publicity posters. The common variations are set out briefly below.

The earliest livery for horse-drawn vehicles appears to have been all-over chocolate, with wheels and shafts often red, and canvas tops and tilts in black. Lettering of various styles appeared, probably in white on canvas covers and in gold on omnibus sides. Harness and brasses were always polished. Later liveries appeared to be more standardised, with cream appearing on upper panelling together with standard GWR lettering. After 1923 the upper panels of van bodies were standardised in cream.

The most common livery for vans, both motor and horse-drawn, became chocolate brown with cream above the waist panel, with the initials 'GWR' in unshaded block serif. Various slogans were carried promoting services. A similar style of lettering – 'GWR' in cream – appeared above the bonnet below the windscreen area. From around 1927 this lettering was replaced by a cast plate lettered 'GWR' and fixed to the cab front and sometimes the radiator. The 'shirt button' monogram was introduced in 1934 and cast plates were removed. Large grey poster panels were painted on van sides. Lining was rare, and roofs were usually left cream but could well be mid-grey, particularly on motor vans.

Open and flat wagons were usually all-over chocolate with cream lettering 'Great Western Railway'. Later, long narrow panels of cream appeared and the lettering within these panels was chocolate. Trailers and horse-drawn flat wagons were generally brown all over, but those used on prestige advertised services had the cream panels. Tarpaulins were black with white lettering and, from 1934, the 'shirt button' emblem was used also in white.

*Above* Morris Commercial lightweight motor parcels van No 1122 in about 1928. The livery is brown, with cream above the waist panel. Note again the combination of electric and oil lamps, the pneumatic tyres, and full windscreen. *Philip J. Kelley collection*

*Below* A Trojan van, Fleet No A1637, at Alfred Road Garage, Westbourne Park, London, on 22 April 1936. The livery is again brown and cream, with the 1934 'shirt button' emblem. Note the easy access from the cab to the rear, and the large grey poster panel on the side. *Philip J. Kelley collection*

A 2-ton Karrier Bantam van, No A2813, photographed at Swindon Works on 16 February 1945. The livery is again brown and cream with the 'shirt button' emblem, but note the white wings and front bumper, and the masked headlight, all to confirm with Second World War blackout conditions. *Philip J. Kelley collection*

# 10
# MODELLING THE
# GREAT WESTERN RAILWAY

The preceding chapters have dealt with the historical development of the Great Western Railway and have highlighted certain characteristics, providing information to enable a reasonable representation of a model based on GWR or BR Western Region practice to be built. We now come to the interesting bit, the construction of a model railway based on the GWR using both this information and the vast source of material available on the company.

Probably the easiest way of describing 'how to' is actually to suggest some layout ideas and to take the reader through their development. There will be no description of the fundamentals of baseboard design, tracklaying or electrics, as these are well covered elsewhere and are of course common to any model railway, not just one based on the Great Western!

Let us start by saying that there is no such thing as a typical Great Western Railway station; indeed, it would be hard to find two in the whole system that had more than a passing resemblance to each other. That said, however, there are only so many basic permutations in authentic track layout design.

The first layout plan (Figure 19) is a very traditional approach to a Great Western branch line terminus and probably owes more to Ashburton in Devon for its inspiration than to anywhere else. The plan shown is, however, not a copy of Ashburton itself, which is not the most convenient of stations to operate, but draws on a number of features from that location.

The setting is the edge of a market town with the emphasis on urban rather than bucolic scenery. The station has an overall roof or train shed, a small engine shed and other features popular with the modeller. The overall size of the layout, including fiddle yard, is 10ft 6in x 1ft

6in in 4mm scale. It could be shortened and made narrower but would possibly suffer visually and, certainly if the width was reduced, lessen the scope for scenic development.

Inevitably any model railway built to suit the sort of space usually available to the modeller will be a compromise and one must accept that short trains and small locomotives must be the order of the day. In any event this is likely to be more in keeping with the type of line portrayed. The layout could also be built in either 2mm or 7mm scales. In the case of the former it would be nice to build it in a space larger than the 5ft 9in minimum in which it could be built, and take advantage of N gauge by creating a railway in the landscape, rather than a layout with some scenery. In 7mm scale, O gauge, the layout would occupy a minimum 18 feet x 2ft 6in, but of course it could be slightly compressed to fit, say, along a garage wall, or even enlarged were more space available.

The design is capable of providing all the typical West Country branch line traffic. The local passenger service would probably be comfortably handled by an auto-coach, steam railmotor, diesel railcar or 'B' set, perhaps strengthened on market days or summer Saturdays to cope with tourist traffic. Freight traffic would consist of the import of coal and manufactured goods and the export of agricultural produce. Cattle and other livestock may require special trains or additional vehicles attached to normal service trains on market days.

There is no 'ready-to-lay' track for GWR two-bolt chair bullhead rail. However, the specialist track component suppliers who primarily cater for 18mm EM or 18-83 S4 gauges supply chairs and parts for hand-built track in 4mm scale, including OO gauge.

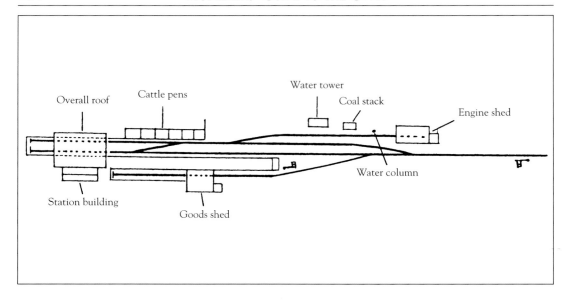

*Above* Figure 19: A branch line terminus based on Ashburton.

*Below* Ashburton station in EM gauge by Chris Lammacraft, the model also illustrated on page 80. The overall roof is shown to good advantage, while on the right are the cattle pens. *Tony Wright, courtesy Model Rail*

*Opposite page* Aerial views of another treatment of Ashburton, this time by John Birkett Smith in N gauge. *Tony Wright, courtesy British Railway Modelling*

The platform is a simple construction project but, if done properly, can help significantly in producing a convincing portrayal of the railway. Platforms come in a variety of constructions; the one suggested is in stone to be compatible with the other structures.

The cattle dock/end-loading facility is really a continuation of the platform and lends itself to similar construction methods. For the cattle pens themselves, square-section plastic drilled to take plastic rod could be used or, alternatively, wooden posts and piano wire. Figure 10 shows the detail of a standard GWR-type cattle dock (see also the photograph on page 43).

Having got the basic 'foundation' structures in place, attention can be turned to the buildings. The non-railway buildings on the layout can come from a variety of sources, at their simplest either from pre-printed card kits supplemented by a printed backscene or, for preference, scratch-built to suit the location. This latter option really is worth the effort and, if based on actual buildings in the area in which the model is set, adds further to the character and atmosphere of the layout. The photographs show some of the buildings that might surround such a station.

The railway buildings consist of the station building, goods shed, engine shed, signal box and the overall roof or train shed. The latter is not available from the trade and will have to be scratch-built, but it is quite a simple task.

The station building, in stone, is a problem as, at the time of writing, only one kit for a stone station building exists, the excellent 4mm scale Ratio 'Castle Cary' building, which will be suitable for a 4mm scale model if the builder does not wish to scratch-build. In any event, this kit includes a canopy that would have to be omitted if the train shed were modelled. In 2mm scale, and indeed 4mm scale, Prototype Models make a number of GWR brick buildings and it would be possible to use these. They could become 'stone built' by overlaying the brickwork with embossed stone card. Modellers in other scales would have to resort to scratch-building.

The train shed would have to be scratch-built as no kits or ready-built examples are available. However, this is not a difficult task, and Figure 20 shows a basic construction utilising plasticard

The goods shed presents a problem similar to that of the station building in respect of available models. An excellent card kit is available for a timber and brick structure from Prototype, which could be used, or a proprietary plastic shed could be modified, detailed and overlaid with embossed plastic stonework in a similar way to the station building. It would not, however, be difficult to scratch-build a suitable structure from plasticard. The primary requirements are a good drawing and patience!

Two kits for engine sheds are available, the Prototype card model based on Tetbury and the Dapol plastic shed. The latter could be overlaid with embossed stone, of course, if the builder wanted all the major structures to be of the same material. A significant improvement can easily be made to card kits by embossing the mortar lines with a sharp, hard lead pencil of 2H or more. Windows too can easily be improved by adding window frames fabricated from plasticard where only printed glazing sheet is provided to represent framing.

Where embossed plastic has been used to represent brick or stonework, careful painting will be well rewarded. Basically, the process consists of flooding the mortar joints with a thin paint of a suitable colour, then wiping this off the top surfaces of the masonry. The masonry should then be given a coat of matt paint to form the base colour for the wall, which can be applied with a large, fairly dry brush to avoid painting the mortar lines. When this is dry, individual bricks and stones can be picked out in slight variations of the base colour on a random basis, or odd examples in a different colour, for example some purple/blue bricks in an otherwise red-brick wall. Moss and fungus growth around gutters and drain pipes can also be added by dry brushing appropriate shades of green.

While on the subject of buildings, there are, particularly in 4mm scale, a significant number of cast and etched parts, ranging from cast columns to decorative cast-iron ridges, available from manufacturers such as Dart Castings and Scale Link, which can be used to detail kits or to assist the scratch-builder by providing some of the more difficult-to-make items of detail. Many typical Great Western Railway features are available and could be successfully incorporated

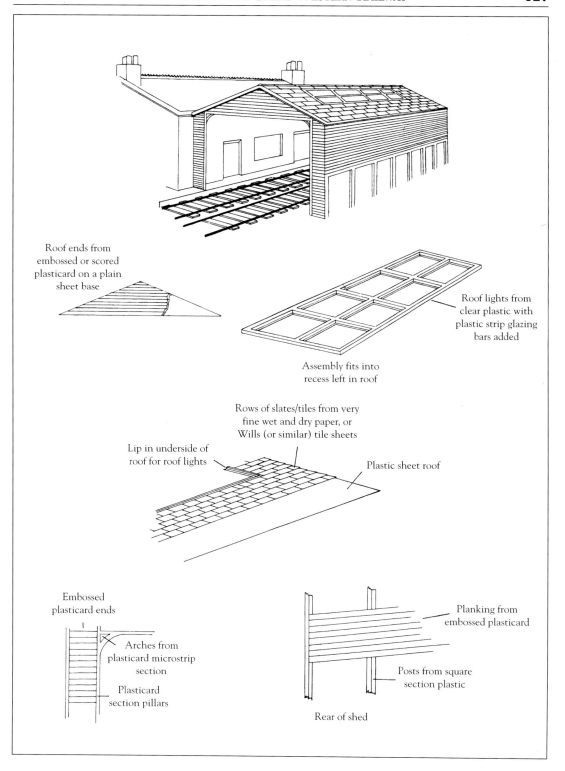

Roof ends from embossed or scored plasticard on a plain sheet base

Roof lights from clear plastic with plastic strip glazing bars added

Assembly fits into recess left in roof

Rows of slates/tiles from very fine wet and dry paper, or Wills (or similar) tile sheets

Lip in underside of roof for roof lights

Plastic sheet roof

Embossed plasticard ends

Arches from plasticard microstrip section

Plasticard section pillars

Planking from embossed plasticard

Posts from square section plastic

Rear of shed

Figure 20: General arrangement of an overall roof and main construction details.

into this layout with advantage. GWR water cranes and the standard conical water tower are available in the three major scales and would ideally be situated close to the shed. Ratio produce in 4mm scale a coal stage, which could also be used. This type of structure could alternatively be scratch-built with ease in other scales with balsa wood for a timber design or from embossed plastic sheet for a brick or stone structure.

The GWR cast-iron spiked railings fence is readily available in the three popular scales as etchings and can be used to good effect around the station. Cast lamps are also available, as are GWR nameboards and a host of other platform accessories.

Signals are available as kits in 2mm, 4mm and 7mm scale. Part-assembled standard working signals are produced by Ratio in 4mm scale and are ideal for this type of layout. Two would be required as shown on the track plan, and ground signals could be incorporated at the loco release crossover in the station. A ground frame from which to work the points and signals would complete the principal structure and two excellent kits are available from Prototype and Ratio in 4mm scale.

There are considerable numbers of detailing parts available to the modeller, from station staff figures to small huts, and the careful use of these will add to the authenticity of the model. Here it is a good idea to browse through the many branch line and photographic albums available to get a 'feel' for the type of scene the model is to portray.

The operation of a station of this nature need not be as dull or restricted as one might imagine. The shed would be a sub-shed of a major shed elsewhere and would stable, and enable light repairs to be made to, the branch passenger engine. Let us assume that a '14XX' and auto-coach provides the branch service. Both would use the shed road for periods between service, while perhaps a freight train is shunted in the yard. Overnight, however, the loco would go to the shed, whereas the coach would be left in the platform road.

The branch freight could be handled by a '45/55XX' Prairie tank, a '57XX' pannier tank, or a Collett '2251' tender loco. Any additional

services, such as cattle trains on market days or special passenger services, would also be handled by similar locos. It would be quite interesting to work out a 'market day' timetable for a branch station such as this; avoiding blocking the platforms or the loco release roads would be a challenge that would have been encountered on the real thing.

If an earlier period were to be modelled, before 1930, the '517' Class 0-4-2s and various saddle tanks or the Metro tank would provide adequate and suitable motive power. Later, perhaps, a diesel railcar would handle passenger workings.

Passenger stock would consist of the auto-coach. An excellent model to diagram A.31 is available in 4mm scale from Hornby, while in N gauge Langley produce a '14XX' and auto-coach kit. In 4mm and 7mm scales a variety of other types are produced in kit form, including railmotor conversions. Excellent AEC diesel railcars are available in 2mm and 4mm scales, ready to run, and an etched brass kit is available in 7mm scale.

Goods stock can be obtained from a variety of sources and if the type of operation mentioned earlier and the comments on freight workings in Chapter 6 are considered, the following should prove adequate:

| | |
|---|---|
| Brake vans | 2 |
| Cattle wagons | 6 |
| Open merchandise wagons | 5 (3 in BR period) |
| Vans | 2 (4 in BR period) |
| Private owner coal/ mineral wagons | 4 (2 wooden-bodied ex-PO and 2 standard 16-ton steel mineral wagons in BR period) |
| Loco coal wagon | 1 |

Additionally, a Siphon, say either a Siphon C, F or G, could be used attached to the passenger working, and a horse-box could also be justified. Additional special wagons may also see occasional use, such as an open carriage truck in an early period setting, say pre-1933, or at any time an implement wagon, or Lowmac, to bring in farm machinery.

The plan in Figure 21 shows an altogether

more comprehensive terminus station, inspired by Kingsbridge. It does not take up too much space and would be ideally suited to a garage or shed location in 4mm scale, but in N gauge could much more easily be accommodated in the average house.

It calls for little comment other than to say that despite its much larger extent, only small 'standard' types of buildings for the station and goods shed are required. The big advantage is that the increased size and capacity of the station allows for larger trains of, say, four coaches, and the use of smaller tender locomotives such as the Churchward 'Moguls', or even a 'Manor', as well as the larger tank locomotives such as the '61XX' Prairies.

The final branch line terminus idea is totally different in concept from the previous examples and is really a light railway (Figure 22). It draws its inspiration from the Culm Valley Light Railway in Devon, and its principal raison d'être is to serve a dairy/creamery. There is also a light

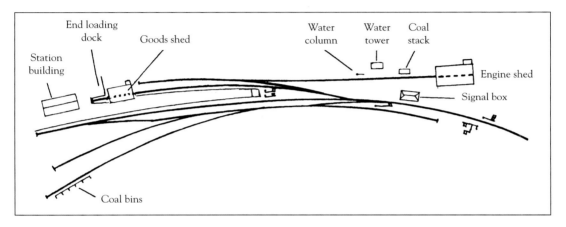

Figure 21: A more comprehensive design of terminus.

Kingsbridge station, inspiration for the layout in Figure 21. An early period layout would enable the use of vintage vehicles, both road and rail, as seen here. *Lens of Sutton*

passenger service and light general freight traffic. It provides, however, the perfect excuse and opportunity to use some of the various Siphons and milk tank wagons, much loved by modellers.

The layout is ideally suited to 4mm or 7mm scale modelling. In 4mm scale the use of finescale bullhead rail trackwork is often considered essential to give the appearance of a lighter-section track.

A small station building, limited goods facilities and a cattle/loading dock are provided, as well of course as the creamery/dairy. The real Culm Valley had buildings designed by one Arthur Pain, who also designed similar buildings for several other smaller railways. Outline drawings of these are provided in Figure 9, and it would be a relatively simple job to scratch-build them from plasticard. However, all is not lost if the builder in 4mm scale does not wish to scratch-build. The goods shed could be represented by the small prefabricated warehouse produced by Ratio and the small

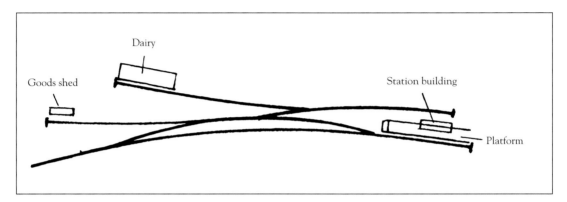

*Above* Figure 22: A light railway terminus.

*Below* Uffculme station on the Hemyock branch, the light railway that inspired the layout in Figure 22. The track layout, buildings and trains are all uncomplicated. *Lens of Sutton*

station building by either the Peco Manyways kit or one of the other 4mm scale kits available for small buildings. The station building need be little more than a small booking office. Additionally, there would be various lamp huts, etc, which would be strategically placed around the station, as well as a ground frame, which could be made from the cast detailing parts available in both 4mm and 7mm scales and which could be located near the edge of the platform. The dairy/creamery could be adapted from one of the many industrial buildings available in kit form.

The remaining details on the layout such as fencing, posters, signs, etc, can be added from the many excellent offerings from the trade. Here the modeller is aided considerably by the detailing parts available from the likes of Dart Castings, P&D Marsh and Langley.

The cattle dock/loading bank could easily be modified from the Ratio model by reducing the number of cattle pens, thus providing the loading bank from part of the platform, though a simple scratch-built affair would be appropriate. A conical water tower could also be utilised at the end of the platform, but preferably a non-GWR type – a simple version is available in 4mm scale from Peco – to emphasise the non-GWR origins of the railway.

The line would definitely be a 'one-engine-in-steam' affair – to be honest there would be little room for a second locomotive – therefore no signalling is required. There would be interesting traffic, the delivery of milk to the dairy/creamery by Siphon and milk tank, some general freight and a limited passenger service. This traffic would be catered for in different ways depending on the period modelled, and some suggestions for appropriate stock are set out below:

**Locomotives:** *1910-1930* '517' Class 0-4-2T, 0-6-0ST. *1930-1964* '57XX' 0-6-0PT, '14XX' Class 0-4-2T. *1964-1970* 'Hymek' or Class 22 diesel for milk traffic, AC railcar for passenger service.

**Coaching stock:** *Up to 1935* Three-coach set of four-wheel vehicles (Ratio in 4mm scale). *1935-1960* Brake 3rd (Collett type). *1960-1968* AC railcar.

**Milk traffic:** *Up to 1930* Open Siphons, such as Siphon C. *After 1930* One or two Siphons, three six-wheel milk tanks (Lima in 4mm scale). *After 1950* Five six-wheel milk tanks (Lima in 4mm scale), CCT short-wheelbase bogie van, perhaps Siphon G.

**General freight:** 2-3 cattle wagons, 2 coal wagons; 1-2 vans for post-1930s period, 3 general merchandise wagons (open), 2 brake-vans

Figure 23 shows three variants of a common track layout for small through branch line stations and concludes our consideration of branch lines.

The plans shown in Figure 24 are for a double-track through station to form the basis for a continuous-run layout. Inevitably these are likely to find more use in 4mm and N gauge than O gauge, where a considerable amount of space would be required for this type of layout.

In N gauge this layout could be built on a hollow interior door (see Figure 24 inset). These can be purchased quite cheaply as 'seconds' and form a lightweight but rigid baseboard. They can be transported easily, in the knowledge that they will fit through a normal doorway without any problem, and can simply be rested on two trestles or, in a more permanent location, arranged to hinge against a wall.

The point motors and wiring can be accommodated quite satisfactorily on the baseboard surface, the former either hidden in buildings or behind a backscene, linkages running in grooves on the baseboard, and the latter being in the form of self-adhesive copper strips.

With a layout of this type there is much more scope for the use of larger buildings and for signalling, signal boxes and railway equipment such as footbridges or stables. The choice of locomotives and rolling-stock becomes unlimited, although this is likely to be governed by the length of train that can be accommodated. After all, a 'King' Class and three coaches would look a little incongruous. The more important aspect of the use of locomotives and stock is to have them in the correct period. Nothing to my mind looks worse on a 'serious' model railway than the incongruity

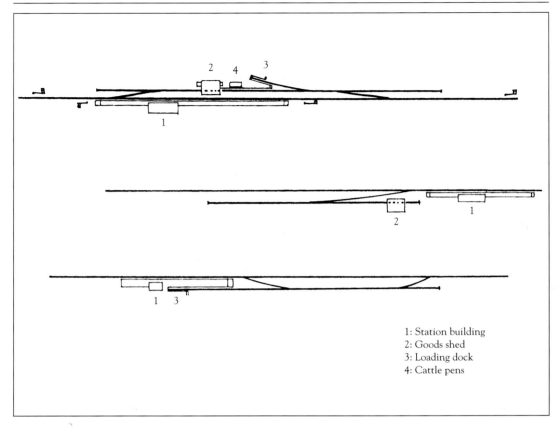

1: Station building
2: Goods shed
3: Loading dock
4: Cattle pens

*Above* Figure 23: Track plans for single-line through stations.

*Below* Figure 24: A double-track station layout, and how it could be accommodated in N gauge on a hollow interior door, as suggested in the text.

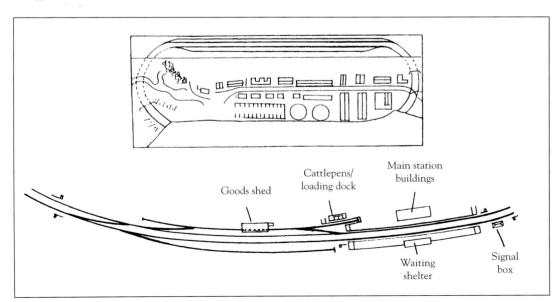

The larger layout allows more scope regarding signalling, structures and train lengths. This is Wellington (Salop) in EM by David Amias. This was a joint GWR/LNWR, later GWR/LMS, station, allowing scope for the modeller who is not totally dyed-in-the-wool GWR to run 'foreign' traffic and employ, as here, upper-quadrant signals. *Tony Wright, courtesy British Railway Modelling*

of a locomotive of one period and stock of another. An extreme but by no means unseen example of this would be a Metro tank on a train of BR Mk 1 coaches, or a 'Western' diesel on a train of pre-war private owner wagons.

There is, however, one very convenient scenario for the modeller who wishes to mix periods and which conveniently suits the builder or collector of locomotives and stock. This is the preserved steam railway. While with a little imagination the basic branch line layouts suggested can be turned into preserved railways, as indeed have real railways, for the minimum of space a steam centre provides an ideal answer.

Chapter 7 outlines briefly the development and types of shed and facilities and includes photographs illustrating sheds and ancillary buildings. Here there is great potential for the modeller to provide the features that are present at these attractions. There is, of course, car parking, a playground, vintage rolling-stock and facilities such as café and gift shop. Taking all this together there is ample opportunity for a variety of authentic modelling in a small space and to run or display whatever takes your fancy.

The operation of such a layout could consist of moving locomotives and stock around the shed and yard area, coaling and watering, and a shuttle with a single carriage or a pair of brake-vans being operated up and down a siding. This latter facility could quite easily be automated.

The Great Western in the 21st century! Authentic former GWR/BR(W) features and atmosphere can be incorporated in a modern image layout, such as Croydon MRS's 'Acton Main Line' in N gauge. *Tony Wright, courtesy Irwell Press*

# APPENDICES

## 1. SELECT BIBLIOGRAPHY

An Historical Survey of Selected Great Western Stations, Volumes 1-3, R. Clark (OPC, 1976)

A Pictorial Record of Great Western Architecture, A. Vaughan (OPC, 1977)

Great Western Branch Line Termini, P. Karau (OPC, combined edition 1985)

GWR Country Stations, Volumes 1 and 2, Chris Leigh (Ian Allan, 1981 and 1984)

An Historical Survey of Great Western Engine Sheds 1837-1947, E. Lyons and E. Mountford (OPC, 1979)

A Pictorial Record of Great Western Signalling, A. Vaughan (OPC, 1973)

A Pictorial Record of Great Western Engines, J. H. Russell (OPC, combined edition 1978)

A Pictorial Record of Great Western Absorbed Engines, J. H. Russell (OPC, 1978)

A Pictorial Record of Great Western Coaches, Parts 1 and 2, J. H. Russell (OPC, 1972 and 1973)

Great Western Coaches Appendix, Volume 1: Standard Passenger Stock, J. H. Russell (OPC, 1981) Volume 2: Special Duty Coaches and the Brown Vehicles, J. H. Russell (OPC, 1984)

Great Western Coaches, Michael Harris (David & Charles, 1972)

A Pictorial Record of Great Western Wagons, J. H. Russell (OPC, 1971)

Great Western Wagons Appendix, J. H. Russell (OPC, 1979)

Great Western Wagons Plan Book, J. H. Russell (OPC, 1972)

A History of GWR Goods Wagons, Volumes 1 and 2, A. G. Atkins (David & Charles, 1976)

All About Iron Minks, J. M. Slinn (HMRS)

Great Western Society
Didcot Railway Centre
Didcot
Oxon OX11 7NJ

Broad Gauge Society
Roger Parkinson, Membership Secretary
9 Strachey Avenue
Old College Park
Leamington Spa
Warks  CV32 6SS

Historical Model Railway Society
Jem Harrison, Secretary
secretary@hmrs.org.uk

## 2. NAMED FREIGHT TRAINS: A SELECTION

### Express vacuum and accelerated 'E' freight trains

| Time | From | To | Name |
|------|------|----|------|
| 1.05am | Acton | Bristol | The High Flyer |
| 3.40am | Banbury Junction | Bristol | The Competitor |
| 2.10am | Basingstoke | Wolverhampton | The Cherbourg |

| Time | From | To | Name |
|------|------|-----|------|
| 3.55pm | Birkenhead | Smithfield | The Meat |
| 9.05pm | Birkenhead | Cardiff | The Mersey |
| 11.00pm | Birmingham | Paddington | The Pedlar |
| 6.50pm | Bristol | Birkenhead | The Farmers Boy |
| 7.40pm | Bristol | Paddington | The 'Bacca' |
| 10.05pm | Bristol | Paddington | The Cocoa |
| 3.50pm | Cardiff | Hanwell Bridge Sidings | The Stock |
| 7.30pm | Carmarthen | Paddington | The Up Welshman |
| 11.00am | Exeter | Pontypool Road | The Ponty |
| 12.05am | Gloucester | Cardiff | The Bacon |
| 7.45pm | Manchester | Bristol | The 'Mon' |
| 4.58pm | Marazion | Bristol | The Tre Pol and Pen Flier |
| 9.32pm | Old Oak Common | Penzance | The Cornishman |
| 10.30pm | Paddington | Cardiff | South Wales Borderer |
| 12.05pm | Paddington | Worcester | The Sauce |
| 2.50pm | Penzance | Paddington | The Searchlight |
| 3.50pm | Swindon | Tavistock Junction | The Rasher |
| 7.35pm | Westbury | Manchester | The Lancashire Lad |
| 10.15pm | Wolverhampton | Westbury | The Crosser |
| 6.45pm | Worcester | Cardiff | The Worcester Fruit |
| 8.35pm | Worcester | Crewe | The 'Sparagras' |

# 3. GOODS WAGON TELEGRAPHIC CODES

| Code name | Description | Diagram No |
|-----------|-------------|------------|
| AERO | Wagon for three-bladed airscrews; trestles aperture in floor | E4 |
| ALE | Converted cattle wagon for beer barrels | V30 |
| ASMO | Passenger motorcar van, vacuum-fitted | G26, 32 |
| BANANA | Formerly FRUIT B | Y.4-7, 12 |
| BEAVER A | Six-wheel flat truck, 20 tons, 18ft | H1 |
| BEAVER B | Six-wheel flat truck, 20 tons, 32ft | H2 |
| BEAVER C | Six-wheel flat truck, 15 tons, 27ft 7in bolsters (later GADFLY) | 16-H5, J10 |
| BEAVER D | Bogie bolster truck (later MACAW G) | J2/3 |
| BEAVER E | Four-wheel flat truck, 20 tons, 20ft | H3-B10 |
| BEETLE | Pedigree cattle truck, vacuum-fitted for passenger train use | W4 |
| BEETLE A | Pedigree cattle truck, dual-braked for passenger train use | W4 |
| BEETLE B | Pedigree cattle truck, vacuum-fitted for goods train use | W4 |
| BEETLE B | Pedigree cattle truck with attendant's compartment, dual-braked for passenger train use | W6/7 |
| BEETLE C | Pedigree cattle truck with attendant's compartment, vacuum-fitted | W6/7/13/14 |
| BLOATER | Large fish van, sliding doors, gas-lit, vacuum fitted | S8-11 |
| BLOATER A | Large fish van, sliding doors, gas-lit, dual-braked | S9-10 |
| BOBOL A (BOGIE BOLSTER A) | Bogie bolster wagon (formerly MACAWs G/H) from 1943 | J2/25/30 |

| Code name | Description | Diagram No |
|---|---|---|
| BOBOL C (BOGIE BOLSTER C) | Bogie bolster wagon (formerly MACAW B) from 1943 | J4/11/14/21/8 |
| BOCAR | Bogie covered wagon (sheeted sides) for motor car bodies, 30 tons | G28/9/30 |
| BOCAR A | Bogie covered wagon (sheeted sides) for motor car bodies, 5 tons | G/33/7/8 |
| BOCAR B | Four-wheel covered wagon (sheeted sides) for motor car bodies, 5 tons | G34/5/6 |
| BORAIL A | From 1943 (formerly MACAW Z) | J27 |
| BORAIL B | From 1943 (formerly MACAW E) | J23 |
| BORAIL C | From 1943 (formerly MACAW C) | J15 |
| BORAIL D | From 1943 (formerly MACAW D) | J22 |
| BORAIL F | From 1943 (formerly MACAW J) | J26/9 |
| CARFIT | From 1943 (formerly SERPENT C) | G21 |
| CARTRUCK | From 1943 (formerly SERPENT and SERPENT C) | G6/9 |
| CARTRUCK A | Formerly SERPENT D | - |
| CEMENT | Cement wagon | V29 |
| CLAY | China clay wagon | O12/13 |
| CONE | Gunpowder van | Z1-4 |
| CONFLAT | Flat wagon for containers, vacuum-fitted | H6-8/10 |
| CONFLAT | Flat wagon for containers | H9 |
| CONFLAT A | Flat wagon for containers, vacuum-fitted, from 1943 | H6-9/10 |
| CORAL | Well wagon for glass in crates | D1 |
| CORAL A | As above with movable partitions | D2 |
| CORDON | Gas truck | DD4/5 |
| CROCODILE | Four-wheel, 34ft, 15 tons | C10 |
| **Note** All Crocodiles were for carrying boilers except where indicated | | |
| CROCODILE A | Four-wheel, 47ft, 15 tons, 1892-98 | - |
| CROCODILE A | 50ft, 25 tons, 1898-1909 | C3 |
| CROCODILE A | 47ft, 15 tons (later 25), from 1909 | C7/13 |
| CROCODILE B | 4ft 6in bogie, 50ft, 20 tons (C3/6 5ft 6in bogie, 52ft, 15 tons in 1909) | C3 (part)/6/11 |
| CROCODILE C | 4ft bogie, 43ft, 35 tons (4ft 6in bogie, 35 tons, 44ft) (C8, 5ft 6in bogie, 47ft, 35 tons in 1903; C1, 5ft 6in bogie, 47ft, 20 tons in 1909) | C1/8 |
| CROCODILE C | 5ft 6in bogie, 52ft, 15 and 20 tons (C3/6, 53ft, 25 tons in 1931/6) from 1909 | C3/4/6 |
| CROCODILE D | 4ft bogie, 33ft, 40 tons (5ft 6in bogie, 87ft, 40 tons in 1906), 1892-1909 | C2 |
| CROCODILE D | 5ft 6in bogie, 47ft, 20 tons (recode to G), 1909-36 | C1 |
| CROCODILE E | 4ft 6in bogie, 44ft, 25 tons, 1898-1909 | C7 |
| CROCODILE E | 5ft 6in bogie, 62ft, 20 (35) tons, from 1909 | C9/15/29 |
| CROCODILE F | 5ft 6in bogie, 52ft, 25 (40) tons (C5, 54ft in 1935) | C3/5/12/20 |
| CROCODILE G | 5ft 6in bogie, 52ft, 25 (40) tons (some 15 (40) tons in 1908), 1902-09 | C4/5 |
| CROCODILE G | 5ft 6in bogie, 47ft, 35 tons, from 1909 | C1/14/16/19/ 22/6 |
| CROCODILE H | 5ft 6in bogie, 37ft, 40 tons, 1908-15 | C13 |

| Code name | Description | Diagram No |
|---|---|---|
| CROCODILE H | 5ft 6in bogie, 42ft 6in, 45 tons (65 tons in 1936), from 1915 | C2/23/7 |
| CROCODILE J | 5ft 6in bogie, 54ft, 40 tons (50 tons in 1923) | C8 |
| CROCODILE K | 5ft 6in bogie, 47ft, 35 tons, 1908-09 | C14 |
| CROCODILE K | 4ft 6in bogie, 46ft, 10 tons (for motor buses), from 1909 | C17 |
| CROCODILE L | 4 x 6 wheel trolley with detachable and interchangeable straight and well-type girders, 86ft 6in, 120 tons | C24/5 |
| CROCODILE M | 5ft 6in bogie, 62ft 6in, 12 (20) tons | C28 |
| DAMO A | Passenger motor car van, 30ft, 2 cars | G24 |
| DAMO B | Passenger motor car van, 20ft, 1 car | G25 |
| DOUBLE | From 1943 (formerly MACAWs A and F) | J7 |
| FISH | Fish van | S2/6/12 |
| FLAT | MACAW E with bolsters, curb rails and stanchions removed | J24 |
| FRUIT | Passenger fruit van, 10ft wheelbase | Y1/2 |
| FRUIT | From 1943 (formerly FRUIT A) | Y1/8/10 |
| FRUIT A | Passenger fruit van, 10ft wheelbase, dual-braked | Y2 |
| FRUIT A | Ventilated goods fruit van | Y1/8/10 |
| FRUIT B | Banana van, steampipe fitted | V8, Y4-7/12 |
| FRUIT C | Passenger fruit van, gas-lit, 22ft, vacuum-fitted | Y3/9 |
| FRUIT D | Passenger fruit van, gas-lit, 22ft, dual-braked | Y3 |
| FRUIT D | Passenger fruit van, gas-lit, 28ft 6in, vacuum-fitted | Y11 |
| GADFLY | Flat trucks for aeroplane traffic | H4/5 |
| GANE | Engineers' 40-ton rail truck, 45ft | J1/13 |
| GANE | Engineers' 40-ton rail truck, 45ft | J1/13 |
| GANE A | Engineers' 40-ton rail truck, 62ft | J26/9 |
| GRAIN | Grain hopper wagon | V20 |
| GRANO | Steel grain hopper | V25 |
| HIGH | Formerly OPEN, new build after 1943 | O5/22/23/24/26/ 31/32/37-40/42 |
| HYBAR | Formerly OPEN A | O2-4/11/14/18/ 22 |
| HYBARFIT | Formerly OPEN B | O2/9/10/15/20/ 22/33/36 |
| HYDRA | Vacuum-fitted passenger well truck for road vehicles | G11/12/13/14/ 19 |
| HYDRA A | As above, unfitted, for use in goods trains | G10/15 |
| HYDRA C | Passenger well truck for motor vehicles, vacuum-fitted | G16 |
| HYDRA D | Passenger well truck for road vehicles, vacuum-fitted | G22 |
| INS (INSUL-MEAT or VENT-INSUL-MEAT | From 1943 (formerly MICAs A and B) | X2/4/5/7-10 |
| INSIXFISH | Refrigerated fish van | S13 |
| LORIOT | Machine truck, no well | G7 |
| LORIOT | Machine well truck, 6 tons, with well | G7 |
| LORIOT A | Machine well truck, 12 tons | G2-4 |
| LORIOT A | Machine well truck, 12 tons | G3 |
| LORIOT B | Machine well truck, 15 tons | G1/18 |
| LORIOT B | Machine well truck, 12 tons | G2 |
| LORIOT C | Machine well truck, 12 tons | G4 |

| Code name | Description | Diagram No |
|---|---|---|
| LORIOT D | Machine well truck, 15 tons, 8ft wide | G1/18 |
| LORIOT E | Machine well truck, 15 tons, 8ft 8in wide | G10 |
| LORIOT F | Machine well truck, 15 tons, ex-Taff Vale Railway | G15 |
| LORIOT G | Machine well truck, 15 tons, ex-Taff Vale Railway | - |
| LORIOT H | Machine well truck, 15 tons, ex-Rhymney Railway | - |
| LORIOT J | Machine well truck, 12 tons, ex-Rhymney Railway | G5 |
| LORIOT K | Machine well truck, 10 tons, ex-Rhymney Railway | G8 |
| LORIOT L | Machine well truck, 15 tons | G13 |
| LORIOT M | Machine well truck, 20 tons | G14 |
| LORIOT N | Machine well truck, 20 tons | G40 |
| LORIOT P | Machine well truck, 20 tons | G42 |
| LORIOT R | Bogie well truck, 25 tons | F4 |
| LORIOT W | Machine well truck, 20 tons | G27/41 |
| LORIOT Y | Machine well truck, 25 tons | G3 |
| MACAW | Four-wheel, single bolster, timber truck, either 9 or 10 tons (some later match trucks) | J8 |
| MACAW A | Four-wheel double bolster timber truck | J7 |
| MACAW B | Bogie bolster rail and timber truck, 30 tons, 45ft | J4/11/14/17-19/ 21/28 |
| MACAW C | Bogie bolster rail and timber truck, 30 tons, 70ft | J15 |
| MACAW D | Bogie flat wagon for tanks, 40 tons, 45ft | J20 |
| MACAW D | Bogie bolster rail and timber truck, 40 tons, 45ft | J22 |
| MACAW E | Bogie bolster rail and timber truck, 30 tons, 45ft | J23 |
| MACAW E | Bogie flat wagon, 30 tons, 45ft | J24 |
| MACAW F | Four-wheel four-bolster timber truck, 10 tons, 25ft (ex-TVR) | - |
| MACAW G | Bogie bolster, 30 tons, 35ft (ex-TVR) | J2 |
| MACAW H | 20-ton bogie bolster, 35ft | J25/30 |
| MACAW J | Bogie bolster, 40 tons, 62ft | J26/29 |
| MACAW Z | Bogie bolster rail and timber truck, 9 tons, 45ft 11in | J27 |
| MAYFLY | Flat truck with well for transformer | G23 |
| MEAT | From 1943 (formerly MICA) | X1/2 |
| MEDFIT | Open wagon with 2 or 3 plank sides | O35 |
| MEX | Cattle truck | W1-3/5 |
| MEX B | Cattle truck, vacuum-fitted | W1/5/8/10-12 |
| MICA | Meat van, ventilated for fresh meat | X1/2/6 |
| MICA A | Refrigerated meat van | X2/3/6/10 |
| MICA B | Refrigerated meat van convertible to ordinary use | X4/5/7/8 |
| MINK A | Covered goods van, 16ft | V4-6/15 |
| MINK B | Covered goods van, 21ft, vacuum-fitted and non-fitted | V2/3 |
| MINK C | Covered goods van, 21ft, ventilated, vacuum-fitted | V7 |
| MINK D | Covered goods van, 28ft 6in, vacuum-fitted | V9/11 |
| MINK F | Bogie goods van, 30 tons, 36ft, later vacuum-fitted | V1 |
| MINK G | Four-wheeled goods van, 20 tons, 30ft, vacuum-fitted | V22 |
| MITE | Twin articulated single bolster timber truck | J9 |
| MITE B | Twin articulated single bolster timber truck | J9 |
| MITE B | Twin articulated single bolster timber truck, 'D' shackles on bolsters | J9 |
| MOGO | Covered goods van with end and side doors, for one motor car | G31/43 |

| Code name | Description | Diagram No |
|---|---|---|
| MOREL | Truck for ship's propellers and large wheels | E1-3 |
| MOREL A | Truck for ship's propellers and large wheels (ex-Barry Railway) | - |
| MOREL B | Truck for ship's propellers and large wheels (ex-Rhymney Railway) | - |
| OPEN | Open wagon | O5/21/23/24/ 26/29/31/32/37 |
| OPEN A | Open wagon with sheet support | O2/4/11/14/18/ 22 |
| OPEN B | Open wagon with sheet support, vacuum fitted | O2/9/10/15/20/ 22/33/36 |
| OPEN C | Open wagon, long wheelbase | O8/16/19/28/ 34 |
| OX | From 1943 (formerly MEX) | W1-3/5 |
| OXFIT | From 1943 (formerly MEX B) | W1/5/8/10/12 |
| PARTO | Covered goods van with movable interior partitions | V26 |
| PASFRUIT | From 1943 (formerly FRUIT) | Y2 |
| PASFRUIT C | From 1943 (formerly FRUIT C) | Y3/9 |
| PASFRUIT D | From 1943 (formerly FRUIT D) | Y11 |
| POLLEN | Small girder or boiler, articulated set of 4 x 4-wheel, 12-ton wagons | A3 |
| POLLEN | Girder or boiler, articulated set of 2 x 4-wheel, 12-ton wagons | A7 |
| POLLEN A | Large girder or boiler, articulated set of 2 x 4-wheel, 20 ton and 2 x 4-wheel, 12-ton wagons | A7 |
| POLLEN A | Girder or boiler, articulated sets of 2 x 4-wheel, 20-ton wagons | A2 |
| POLLEN B | Girder or boiler, articulated sets of 2 x 4-wheel, 30-ton wagons | A1 |
| POLLEN C | Girder or boiler, articulated sets of 2 x 4-wheel, 20-ton wagons | A4 |
| POLLEN D | Girder or boiler, articulated sets of 2 x 4-wheel, 20-ton wagons | A5 |
| POLLEN E | Large gun, girder or boiler, articulated set of 4 x 6-wheel, 30-ton wagons | A6/8 |
| POLLEN E | Girder articulated set (part of above), 2 x 6-wheel, 30-ton wagons | A9/10 |
| RECTANK | Bogie machinery trolley (ex-WD), some later with bolsters | C21, J31 |
| RODER | Flat truck for road vehicles | G10 |
| SERPENT | For agricultural machines, furniture vans, 17ft or 18ft | G6-9 |
| SERPENT A | For agricultural machines, 15 tons, 28ft | G5 (originally), B5 |
| SERPENT B | For agricultural machines, 20 tons, 23ft | G5 (originally), B4 |
| SERPENT C | For agricultural machines, 12 tons, 18ft, vacuum-fitted | G21 |
| SERPENT D | For agricultural machines, 10 tons, 21ft 3in (ex-TVR) | - |
| SHOCVAN | Shock-absorbing van | V27/28 |
| SINGLE | From 1943 (formerly MACAW) | J8 |
| TADPOLE | Open fish truck for passenger train use | S1-7 |
| TADPOLE | Open fish truck (4 and 6-wheel) for passenger train use | S4-7 |
| TADPOLE A | Open fish truck with guard's compartment, 6-wheel and bogie, for passenger train use | S2/3/5 |
| TADPOLE A | Bogie open fish trucks, for passenger train use | S1-3 |
| TEVAN | Converted MICAs A and B for specific traffics, eg Lyons, Frys | V31/32 |

| Code name | Description | Diagram No |
|---|---|---|
| TOAD | Goods brake-van (including PW and Plough vans) | AA1-23 (excl AA7/9/10) |
| TOAD A | Goods brake-van, vacuum-fitted | AA2/5/7/9/10/ 11/13/15/20/21 |
| TOADFIT | From 1943 (formerly TOAD A) | |
| TOTEM | Bogie (3 bogies, 12 wheels), armour plate, ingot or roll wagon, 45 tons | B1 |
| TOTEM A | Bogie (2 bogies, 8 wheels), armour plate, ingot or roll wagon, 45 tons (later 50 tons) | B2 |
| TOTEM B | Six-wheel armour plate wagon, 30 tons (ex-Rhymney Railway) | B6 |
| TOURN | Bogie open truck, 25 tons, 36ft | O1 |
| TRAVAN | Covered goods van, capacity greater than 12 tons, formerly MINKs B, F and G | V1/2/22 |
| TUBE | From 1943 (formerly OPEN C) | O8/16/19/28/ 34/41 |
| TWIN | From 1943 (formerly MITE and MITE B) | J9 |
| VAN | From 1943 (formerly MINK and MINK A) | V4-6/12/15/16/ 18/21/24/33-35/ 37/38 |
| VANFIT | As above, vacuum-fitted | V3/7/9/11/12/ 14/18/19/21/ 23/36 |

# 4. LOCOMOTIVE HEADLAMP CODES

A  Express passenger trains
B  Ordinary passenger trains and mixed trains
C  Livestock or perishable traffic trains (coaching stock) and express freight trains (vacuum brake fitted stock); also trains of empty coaching stock
E  Livestock or perishable traffic (goods stock) and freight trains (Class A)
F  Express livestock and freight trains (Class B)
G  Light engines
H  Freight trains: through loads to destination
J  Freight trains: stopping intermediately
K  Ordinary freight trains

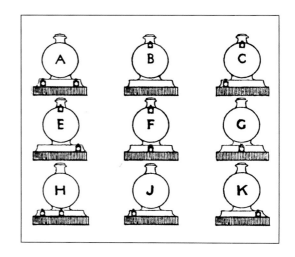

From the GWR publication *The Cheltenham Flyer* (1934)

# 5. GWR STANDARD SIGNALLING BELL-CODES

**Beats**

Call Attention                1
(Emergency call attention: a number of beats
in rapid succession)

**'Is Line Clear' for:**

Express passenger train, express diesel railcar,
breakdown van train going to clear the line,
'light engine' going to assist disabled train,
empty coaching stock timed at express speed
('A' headlamps)                4

Ordinary passenger train, 'mixed' train,
breakdown van train not going to clear the
line? ('B' headlamps)          3-1

Branch passenger train (only on main line
to junction)? ('B' headlamps)   1-3

Rail motor-car, auto-train or streamline
railcar? ('B' headlamps)        3-1-3

Parcels, newspaper, fish, meat, fruit, horse,
cattle or perishable train composed entirely
of vacuum-fitted stock with the vacuum pipe
connected to the engine? ('D' headlamps)    5

Express freight, livestock, perishable or
ballast train partly vacuum fitted with not
more than one-third vacuum-braked
vehicles connected by vacuum pipe to the
engine? ('D' headlamps)         4-4

Express freight, or ballast train conveying a
stipulated number of vacuum-braked
vehicles connected by vacuum pipe to the
engine and authorised to run at a
maximum speed of 35mph?         2-2-3

Empty coach stock not specially
authorised to carry 'A' headlamps?
('D' headlamps)                 2-2-1

Express freight, fish, meat, fruit or cattle
train, ballast train or breakdown van train
not proceeding to an accident ('E'
headlamps)                      3-2

Through fast freight train conveying
through load? ('F' headlamps)   1-4

**Beats**

Light engine or light engines coupled
together or engine and brake-van? ('G'
headlamps)                      2-3

Freight, mineral or ballast train or train of
empties carrying through load to
destination? ('H' headlamps)    3-4-1

Freight, mineral or ballast train stopping at
intermediate stations? ('J' headlamps)    3

Train conveying out-of-gauge or
exceptional load? ('J' headlamps)    2-6-2

Branch freight train (only on main line to
junction)? ('K' headlamps)      1-2

Ballast train, freight train or inspection
train requiring to stop in section?
('K' headlamps)                 1-2-2

Trolley requiring to go into or pass
through tunnel?                 2-1-2

Train approaching               1-2-1

Train entering section          2

Section clear but station or junction
blocked                         3-5-5

Line clear to clearing point only    2-2-2

Engine assisting in rear of train    2-2

Train out of section, or obstruction
removed                         2-1

Engine arrived                  2-1-3

Train drawn back clear of station    3-2-3

Blocking back inside home signal    2-4

Blocking back outside home signal    3-3

Blocking back outside home signal for
train already in section        1-2-3

Shunt train for following train to pass    1-5-5

Opening signal box              5-5-5

Closing signal box              7-5-5

Testing bells                   16

Time signal                     8-5-5

| | Beats |
|---|---|
| | **Beats** |
| Lampman or fogman required | 9-5-5 |
| Testing slotted signal | 5-5-5-5 |
| Take off slot train waiting | 3-4 |
| Cancel 'Is Line Clear?' | 3-5 |

**Emergency bell signals:**

| | Beats |
|---|---|
| Obstruction danger | 6 |
| Stop and examine train | 7 |

| | Beats |
|---|---|
| Train passed without tail lamp | |
| To box in advance | 9 |
| To box in rear | 4-5 |
| Train divided | 5-5 |
| Train or vehicles running away on right line | 4-5-5 |
| Train or vehicles running away on wrong line | 2-5-5 |

# INDEX